THE
DOMINGUEZ FAMILY

A MEXICAN-AMERICAN JOURNEY

*One Family's Struggle to
Find Its Place in America*

Donna S. Morales
and
John P. Schmal

HERITAGE BOOKS
2012

HERITAGE BOOKS

AN IMPRINT OF HERITAGE BOOKS, INC.

Books, CDs, and more—Worldwide

For our listing of thousands of titles see our website
at
www.HeritageBooks.com

Published 2012 by
HERITAGE BOOKS, INC.
Publishing Division
100 Railroad Ave. #104
Westminster, Maryland 21157

Copyright © 2004 Donna S. Morales and John P. Schmal

Other Heritage Books by Donna S. Morales and John P. Schmal:

Mexican-American Genealogical Research: Following the Paper Trail to Mexico

The Dominguez Family: A Mexican-American Journey

The Indigenous Roots of a Mexican-American Family

Other Heritage Books by John P. Schmal:

Naturalizations of Mexican Americans: Extracts, Volumes 1–4

The Journey to Latino Political Representation

Other Heritage Books by John P. Schmal and Jennifer Vo:

A Mexican-American Family of California: In the Service of Three Flags

Cover photo: Pfc. Louis Dominguez, 1944

International Standard Book Numbers
Paperbound: 978-0-7884-2527-1
Clothbound: 978-0-7884-9434-5

DEDICATION

This work is dedicated to two soldiers who
defended America in her darkest hours during
World War II:

Erminio Dominguez,
Pfc., 117th Mechanized Division (Cavalry)
POW, Stalag 7A (Moosburg, Germany)

And

Louis Dominguez
Pfc., 75th Infantry Division
Killed in action, March 31, 1945
Papen, Germany

TABLE OF CONTENTS

TABLE OF CONTENTS

TABLE OF CONTENTS

TABLE OF CONTENTS

ILLUSTRATIONS

ACKNOWLEDGEMENTS

We would not have been able to put this story together without the help of Esperanza Rangel Amayo. Her childhood friendship with Louis Dominguez provided us with some insight into the lives of the Dominguez family and other Mexican-American families living in Kansas City during the pre-World War II era. Esperanza's dedication to the cause of getting recognition for Mexican-American contributions to Kansas City is admirable, and we cannot thank her enough for helping us put this story together.

Other people living in the Kansas City area who provided us with information were Louie Gonzales and Carole Turner. Carole did some research for us and introduced us to Esperanza, while Louie provided us with both pictures and details about the Dominguez family history. Louie provided us with the picture of Geronimo Dominguez and his children. He also gave us the 1917 picture of the Dominguez children. In addition, we offer a gracious thanks to Jesse Dominguez and Bessie Dominguez Morales for sharing some of their experiences with us.

ACKNOWLEDGEMENTS

The works of Professor Valerie Mendoza and Cynthia Mines helped us to paint a picture of Mexican-American life in Kansas during the early decades of the Twentieth Century. Without their works, we would have had difficulty understanding the early Mexican-American community of Kansas City.

Steve Graber and Jacque Stoltz – a veteran of the 75th Infantry Regiment during World War II – procured the diary of Louie Dominguez's A Company. And the memoirs of the ex-POW Bill Ethridge (*Time Out. A Remembrance of World War II*) gave us a vivid picture of General George S. Patton's liberation of Stalag VII-A, during which Erminio Dominguez became a free man after eight months in German captivity.

We would also like to thank our friend, Eddie Martinez, who helped us with several of the illustrations. And finally, we thank the Immigration and Naturalization Service (INS) for publishing very useful statistics on Mexican immigration.

INTRODUCTION

The United States has been a major destination for many immigrants over the last two centuries. And each immigrant group – upon its arrival on American shores or at American ports of entry – has had a unique experience. When a family finds it necessary to move from one country to another, the cultural and emotional bond to the birthplace usually remains very strong. As a result, there is some reluctance to change allegiance or adapt to the culture and the tradition of the new country.

But – at some point – the immigrant family comes to realize that they will probably never return to their former home. And they also begin to understand that their livelihood and well-being may be contingent on their ability to adapt to the new lifestyle in their new home. As children are born, they become a new generation of citizens of a new country and they are likely to be assimilated into the dominant culture. And all of these factors sever the ties to the native land over time.

INTRODUCTION

Such has been the dilemma for millions of Mexican families that have made their way north over the last century. And the great majority of these people believed that their lives had improved significantly and decided to stay in the United States. Such was the case for my family – the Dominguez family of Kansas City, Kansas.

The Dominguez family lived in the Mexican state of Zacatecas. But during the first decade of the Twentieth Century, the entire Mexican Republic was suffering from drought, economic depression, political upheaval and serious social inequities. So, like thousands of other Mexican laborers, they decided to move north in the hope of procuring gainful employment with the Mexican railroads. But in a nation sitting on the brink of a devastating civil war and social chaos, moving north was not enough.

INTRODUCTION

In 1909, my great-grandfather – Aniceto Dominguez – brought his family across the border at El Paso, Texas. By this time, many of the railroad companies had begun to see Mexican laborers as loyal, hard-working and compliant employees. Even a low wage railroad job in the United States paid three to five times more than the equivalent Mexican job.

First, the Dominguez family moved to the Texas Panhandle and – with the labor shortages caused by World War I being a strong incentive – moved on to Kansas City. Our services in the railroad and meat packing industries of Kansas City were very much desired by the Kansas business community. However, from a social standpoint, my family was not eagerly nor warmly welcomed to Kansas during the early decades of the Twentieth Century.

For the first decades of our stay in Kansas, we endured discrimination, humiliation, and segregation at the hands of our own countrymen. We could not eat at certain restaurants, could not attend certain church services, were not allowed in some movie theaters and could not send our children to certain schools.

But our family – like many Mexican-American families – could not envision returning to a land that had become foreign to them. So we made the best of it and decided to fight for our piece of the pie. All adult members of my family found gainful employment and became involved in church and civil activities. And when World War II came, our family did not hesitate to play its role.

My family is a patriotic family and, like many other American families, we have made sacrifices for the country we love. My Uncle Louis Dominguez paid for the freedom of all Americans with his life while fighting against the tyranny of Adolph Hitler. My Uncle Erminio Dominguez also served his country with distinction and endured the humiliation and terror of being

INTRODUCTION

captured by Nazi forces while defending a small town in France against a German counterattack.

The story of the Dominguez family is a complex story. The lives we led in earlier centuries are remarkably different from the lives we lead today. Our journey has taken many twists and turns through history and from the silver mines of Zacatecas to the railroad yards of Kansas and the battlegrounds of Europe.

My family has been in the United States for almost a century and in that period of time, we have earned an important place in American society. Through our endurance, faith and hard work, we have been able to stake our claim to the American dream. My feelings about my family's accomplishments can be best summarized through the words of Dominguez family friend, Esperanza Amayo, a Kansas City resident who has contributed articles about the experiences, tribulations, and contributions of the Mexican-American community to Kansas. In an interview

INTRODUCTION

with us, Esperanza explained that "we [Mexican Americans in Kansas] have contributed in war and in peace to the productivity and stability of this community and now enjoy a self-fulfilling and respectable place in its society."

IN SEARCH OF A NEW LIFE

The Journey North

December 18, 1909. The railroad train made its way north along the *Ferrocarriles Nacionales de México* (National Railroad of Mexico) in the cool night air of the Chihuahua Desert. It was late in the afternoon as 25-year-old Geronimo Dominguez and his wife Luisa Lujan – and other migrants from the south – watched the desert landscape from their passenger car.

Geronimo carefully guided the steps of Luisa, who carried their infant daughter, Felicitas. Four months earlier, on August 9, 1909, Luisa had given birth to Felicitas, in the state of Durango. However, giving birth would always be a trial for Luisa, and her recoveries were always long and difficult. So, as they rode the railways northward toward the border town of Ciudad Juárez, Luisa was still weak and frail.

With a sickly wife and a newborn child to support, Geronimo hoped to catch up with his father, Aniceto Dominguez, who had

1

crossed the border into the United States a month earlier on November 19. Aniceto had crossed the international line with his wife, his three children, and Geronimo's four-year-old son Pablo. Now Aniceto waited with his family in El Paso for the arrival of his son's family so that they could move on to their next destination in the interior of Texas.

In the first decade of the Twentieth Century, American railroad companies were actively recruiting many Mexican laborers. The American railroads looked for inexpensive laborers from Mexico to help build and maintain their tracks. Since American immigration laws enacted in the late 1800s had restricted the influx of Chinese and Japanese laborers, Mexican workers were now in great demand. Many of the German and Irish immigrants who arrived in the Southwestern U.S. during these years sought more profitable jobs in other industries, so the railroads found their most willing and able laborers in the Mexican migrants who were crossing the border in ever-increasing numbers looking for gainful employment.

In 1909, some railroads even sponsored employment agencies that met with the Mexican nationals as they crossed the border from Ciudad Juárez into El Paso, Texas. As a matter of fact, in the previous year, some 16,000 Mexicans had been recruited in El Paso for railroad work. And, by 1910, 2,000 Mexican citizens were crossing the border each month for railroad work.[1] Once employed, a Mexican laborer could receive transportation to a new job and residence in an American state, far from the instability and problems that had begun surface in his native land.

The most vigorous employer and recruiter of Mexican laborers in the first decade of the Twentieth Century was the Atchison,

---

[1] Carey McWilliams, *North From Mexico: The Spanish-Speaking Peoples of the United States* (New York: Greenwood Press, 1968), pp. 167-169.

IN SEARCH OF A NEW LIFE

Topeka and Santa Fe Railroad (AT&SF), more popularly known as "the Santa Fe." When the Santa Fe Railroad approached Aniceto, he recognized that he would now have the opportunity to lead his family to what he believed would be a better life in a new land.

Geronimo Dominguez and Luisa Lujan were my maternal grandparents, and Aniceto Dominguez was my great-grandfather. The reasons that Aniceto Dominguez and his family had to leave their homes in northwestern Zacatecas are not entirely clear. But one thing is very clear: Like many lower class Mexican citizens, Aniceto had found himself at the mercy of the hacienda owners near Río de Medina in the municipio of Sain Alto, Zacatecas.

It is believed that Aniceto had not offered the proper deference reserved for a hacienda jefe, and – as a result – Aniceto had become persona non grata in his own native land. In effect, the

Dominguez family joined the ranks of the nine million landless peons living throughout the Mexican Republic.

Aniceto and Geronimo had both married their respective wives in Zacatecas in late 1903. For Aniceto this was his second marriage, following the death several years earlier of his first wife, Martina Segovia (Geronimo's mother and my great-grandmother). Soon after, the Dominguez family left the Hacienda de Santa Monica outside of Sain Alto for another hacienda, Paso de la Cruz, several miles to the southeast. Then, in 1906, both Geronimo and Aniceto had gone north to the twin cities of Gómez Palacios and Torreón where they found employment with the railroads.

The Laguna District

Torreón, located on the Nazas River in the southern part of the state of Coahuila, was founded in 1893 and quickly developed into one of the most important commercial and railway centers of Northern Mexico. Torreón's sister city of Gómez Palacio – in the neighboring state of Durango – had also been founded in 1893. Both cities are part of the Laguna District, which is one of several drainage basins of the Central Mexican Plateau.

The formidable Mexican Plateau is surrounded by the Sierra Madre Oriental (on the east side) and the Sierra Madre Occidental (on the west side). Its drainage basins – including the Laguna District – have no outlet to either ocean. As a result, the Laguna District became a major agricultural center with the introduction of large-scale irrigation along the Nazas River.

The development of Laguna's commerce was further enhanced by the construction of railways that facilitated the delivery of agricultural products to markets throughout the country. By the early part of the Twentieth Century, two major railway lines already connected the City of Torreón with Ciudad Juárez, 831 kilometers (516 miles) to the northwest. This strategic connection with the northern border turned the both Torreón and the Laguna District into major transportation and commercial hubs.

In these early years, the rapid construction of the Mexican railroads offered new opportunities to poor Mexican laborers from small towns. This fast and relatively cheap form of transportation enabled an unemployed laborer to rapidly make his way to urban or agricultural areas to find employment. Thus, the railroads going into Torreón started drawing large numbers of laborers from the adjacent states, including Zacatecas.

For the convenience of our readers, we have reproduced on the following page a 1925 map from the Department of Commerce's *Trade Promotion Series No. 16*,[2] showing the route of the Ferrocarriles Nacionales de México (National Railroad of Mexico) through Chihuahua to the border area.

---

[2] W. Rodney Long, *Railways of Mexico* – Department of Commerce, Bureau of Foreign and Domestic Commerce Trade Promotion Series No. 16 (Washington, D.C.: Government Printing Office, 1925).

The Railroads Through Chihuahua

IN SEARCH OF A NEW LIFE

It was the National Railroad – going north from Torreón – that led my grandparents through central Chihuahua to Ciudad Juárez and El Paso and a new life in America.

Economic Decline

In better times, many Mexican men may not have been so anxious to leave their families to work in a strange city fifty or one hundred miles away from home. However, starting in 1903, several sectors of the Mexican economy had begun to decline steadily. First of all, Mexico's production of foodstuffs – so dependent upon the labor-intensive hacienda system – began to stagnate and could not keep pace with the growth of the population. As a result, per capita production began to decline.

Soon after, Mexico's mining industry – so important to Zacatecas – also began to decline. By 1907, a serious economic depression, accompanied by a devastating three-year drought (1907-1909), had severe repercussions that left thousands of migrant workers in Zacatecas and neighboring states without jobs.

Initially, the Laguna District provided some relief for the chronic labor shortages that accelerated with each month. But a succession of poor harvests in northern Mexico – caused by both droughts and floods – provoked a significant increase in the price of corn and beans, which led to a sharp increase in the cost of living after 1906.[3] Even as corn tripled in price, the wages of most laborers remained static, making it difficult for many Mexican families to put food on the table.

---

[3] The labor problems in the Laguna District during these years are discussed in some detail by David W. Walker, "Homegrown Revolution: The Hacienda Santa Catalina del Alamo and Agrarian Protest in Eastern Durango, Mexico, 1897-1913," Hispanic American Historical Review (May 1992), pp. 239-273.

IN SEARCH OF A NEW LIFE

Today, most analysts believe that the Depression of 1907-1909 "erased a decade of upward mobility" and led directly to the overthrow of the Mexican President Porfirio Díaz.[4] By 1909, the rumblings of social and economic discontent could be detected at many levels of Mexican society.

The Decision

Life is always full of important decisions. But few decisions have such great consequence as the decision of a man to leave his native land and bring his family to a new life in another country. Nineteen hundred and nine was a turning point for my family. On a cool December day, my grandparents Geronimo and Luisa embarked on their journey north and did not look back.

---

[4] Mark Wasserman, *Everyday Life and Politics in Nineteenth Century Mexico: Men, Women, and War* (Albuquerque: The University of New Mexico Press, 2000), pp. 169, 225.

IN SEARCH OF A NEW LIFE

In crossing the border at El Paso, Geronimo and Luisa were dramatically altering the destiny of their entire family. If, for some reason, Geronimo had chosen to stay in Mexico, there is no telling what would have happened to him and his family. And if Geronimo and Aniceto had returned to Zacatecas, it is very possible that they may have become statistics in one of the longest and bloodiest civil wars of the Twentieth Century.

Within the next year, the first shots of the Mexican Revolution would be heard throughout the land. This Civil War between various factions of Mexican society would tear the fabric of Mexican life from one end of the country to another. And, by the time the war had ended (1920), one in eight Mexican citizens would be dead. Would my family have survived this catastrophic event?

Because Grandmother Luisa was too weak to travel after the birth of my Aunt Felicitas, my great-grandfather Aniceto Dominguez brought his family and four-year-old nephew Pablo north to El Paso in the late fall of 1909, while Geronimo stayed in the south with Luisa and Felicitas. On November 17, Aniceto crossed the border with his family.

Even in these days, El Paso – as a railroad communications center – was the most important city for the distribution of Mexican immigrants into the United States. Here, Mexican laborers were met by representatives of American employment agencies, who would usually advance board, lodging and transportation to a place where work was available.[5]

Once his wife and child were well enough to travel, Geronimo brought both Luisa and Felicitas north, crossing the border on December 19, 1909. Both Dominguez families quickly made their way by railroad to the city of Canadian in Hemphill County, Texas. Canadian, located in the rolling plains on the eastern edge

---

[5] Cynthia Mines, *Riding the Rails to Kansas* (Kansas: 1980), p. 34.

of the Texas Panhandle near the border of Oklahoma, was a stop along the Santa Fe Railroad, a company that would employ many members of my family in decades to come. It was this railroad center, 120 miles northeast of Amarillo, that had encouraged settlement of the area for two decades and it was here that my family made its first American home.

This was the beginning of our American journey, one that would include segregation, discrimination, hard work, and sorrow. But this experience also included service to God, church, community, and country. And it is through this service that our family earned its place in American society. It was a difficult process because – at first – we were not warmly welcomed by our neighbors and fellow citizens. But in time, our labor, our faith, and our patriotism would earn the respect of the community. On the following pages, we will tell our story.

ZACATECAS: A DEFIANT LAND

Zacatecas

My family has made its home in Kansas City for the better part of the last century. But before 1909, the Dominguez family lived for many generations in the municipio of Sain Alto in the Mexican state of Zacatecas. The State of Zacatecas shares common borders with Coahuila de Zaragoza (on the north), Nuevo León and San Luis Potosí (on the east), Guanajuato, Jalisco and Aguascalientes (on the south) and Nayarit on the west.

Zacatecas, which occupies 3.8% of the total surface of the Mexican Republic, is the eighth largest state in Mexico with a total of 75,040 square kilometers (following Tamaulipas, Jalisco, Oaxaca, Durango, Coahuila, Sonora, and Chihuahua).[1] Politically, the state is divided into fifty-six municipios – the rough equivalent of our American counties – and has a total of 5,064 localities, 86% of which correspond to the old haciendas.

---

[1] Instituto Nacional de Estadística Geografía e Informática (INEGI), *Superficies Nacionales y Estatales* (Mexico: 1999).

ZACATECAS: A DEFIANT LAND

With a population of 1,353,610 inhabitants in 2000,[2] Zacatecas depends upon cattle raising, agriculture, mining, communications, tourism, and transportation for its livelihood. Although much of Zacatecas is desert, the primary economic driver of the state is agriculture, which utilizes 27.38% of the state area and accounts for 25.14% of the state's economic activity.[3]

Zacatecas is Mexico's foremost producer of beans, chili peppers and cactus leaves, and holds second place in guava production, third in grapes, and fifth in peaches. Livestock raising – including both cattle and sheep – and food processing are also important components of Zacatecas' economy.

---

[2] INEGI. *Tabulados Básicos. Estados Unidos Mexicanos. XII Censo General de Población y Vivienda, 2000* (México, 2001).

[3] INEGI, *Carta de Uso del Suelo y Vegetación*, 1:250 000.

ZACATECAS: A DEFIANT LAND

The Silver Industry

Silver, tin, lead, copper and gold mining are also important economic activities in the state of Zacatecas. As a matter of fact, Zacatecas is Mexico's main silver producer, second in lead and tin production, and fourth in gold production. It was the mining industry that first brought fame and fortune to Zacatecas in the Sixteenth Century. As a matter of fact, thanks to Zacatecas, even today Mexico is the largest producer of silver in the world, contributing 17% of the world's total output, followed closely by Peru, and more distantly by Australia and the United States.

Zacatecas, as the number one silver-producing state of Mexico, contains fifteen major mining districts, the most famous of which are near the cities of Fresnillo and Zacatecas. Other metals and minerals produced in the state include zinc, copper, mica, fluorite, barium, mercury, bentonite, and non-metallic phosphorus.

ZACATECAS: A DEFIANT LAND

The story of silver dominates the history of Zacatecas from the first arrival of the Spaniards and their Indian allies from southern Mexico. On September 8, 1546, Juan de Tolosa, a Basque of noble heritage, leading a small force of Spaniards and Indian auxiliaries, met up with a group of Zacatecos Indians near the site of the present-day capital city of Zacatecas. Tolosa and the natives exchanged some gifts in this friendly confrontation. It was later determined that some of the trinkets that the Indians had given to Tolosa were silver. At a later day, the Indians took Tolosa to the location of the ore deposits. This encounter marks the beginning of Zacatecas' famous and profitable silver industry.[4]

Soon after, Spanish settlers founded the small town of Zacatecas as an outpost in the area. When a rich vein of silver ore was discovered at nearby Veta Grande, a great rush began towards the

---

[4] P.J. Bakewell, *Silver Mining and Society in Colonial Mexico: Zacatecas, 1546-1700.* (Cambridge: Cambridge University Press, 1971), p. 22; J. Lloyd Mecham, *Francisco de Ibarra and Nueva Vizcaya* (Durham, North Carolina: Duke University Press, 1927), pp. 41-42; Martha Menchaca, *Reconstructing History, Constructing Race: The Indian, Black, and White Roots of Mexican Americans* (Austin: University of Texas Press, 2001), p. 75.

small settlement. However, Zacatecas itself did not earn the title of city until October 8, 1585, when King Felipe II of Spain granted it the title of "Very Noble and Loyal City of Our Lady of Zacatecas."[5]

The discovery of rich mineral-bearing deposits in this area put the spotlight on Zacatecas. The spotlight grew wider as other deposits were discovered farther north: San Martín (1556), Chalchihuites (1556), Avino (1558), Sombrerete (1558), Fresnillo (1566), Mazapil (1568), and Nieves (1574). According to late historian, John Lloyd Mecham, "The growth of Zacatecas was phenomenal. The news of the rich discoveries spread rapidly, and soon the region was crowded with treasure seekers... From 1548 to 1810 Zacatecas produced in silver five hundred and eighty-eight million dollars."[6]

---

[5] Philip Wayne Powell, *Soldiers, Indians and Silver; North America's First Frontier War* (Tempe, Arizona: Center for Latin American Studies, Arizona State University, 1975), pp. 157-158.

[6] J. Lloyd Mecham, *op. cit.*, p.46.

ZACATECAS: A DEFIANT LAND

The Zacatecas Resistance

For over three hundred years, my ancestors in Zacatecas lived, worked, and served under the flags of Spain and Mexico. As Christians, they baptized their children and took their marriage vows in the Catholic churches that the Spaniards had built on their ancestral lands. For three centuries, my ancestors had been fully integrated into the central Hispanic culture and as laborers they represented an integral part of the Spanish colonial economy.

However, I recognize that a large part of my family's Zacatecas heritage belongs to the aboriginal peoples who originally inhabited Zacatecas, long before the Spaniards reached the shores of Mexico in 1519. Four-and-a-half centuries ago, when the Spaniards first entered Zacatecas, my Indian ancestors resisted with a ferocity that became legendary. After the initial silver strike in 1546, managing and exploiting the mineral wealth of Zacatecas had become a very difficult task for the Spanish entrepreneurs. For the next half-century, the indigenous inhabitants of Zacatecas waged a fierce and intense guerrilla war against the Spaniards and their Indian allies.

The Chichimeca Indians

The definitive source of information relating to the Chichimeca Indians and the Chichimeca War of the second half of the Sixteenth Century is Philip Wayne Powell's *Soldiers, Indians, and Silver: North America's First Frontier War.* Dr. Powell tells us that that the term Chichimeca "was an all-inclusive epithet" that had "a spiteful connotation." This designation, learned by the Spaniards from the Aztecs, was applied to the multitude of tribes inhabiting the north central section of Mexico.[7]

The lands inhabited by the Chichimeca Indians came to be known as the Gran Chichimeca. The primary tribes occupying this territory were the Zacatecos, the Pames, the Guamares, and the

---

[7] Philip Wayne Powell, *op. cit.*, p. 33; Martha Menchaca, *op. cit.*, pp. 38-39.

ZACATECAS: A DEFIANT LAND

Guachichiles. All of the Chichimeca Indians shared a primitive hunting-collecting culture, based on the gathering of mesquite and tunas (the fruit of the nopal). However, many of them also lived off of acorns, roots and seeds. In some areas, they even cultivated maize and some calabashes. From the mesquite they made white bread and wine. Many Chichimec tribes utilized the juice of the agave as a substitute for water when the latter was in short supply.

On the following page is a map indicating the primary indigenous groups that inhabited the state of Zacatecas at the time the Spaniards arrived in the area. Our illustrator Eddie Martinez has indicated the approximate boundaries of the various Chichimec nations. However, because many of these tribes were warlike, intrusions by one tribe into another tribe's territory were commonplace.

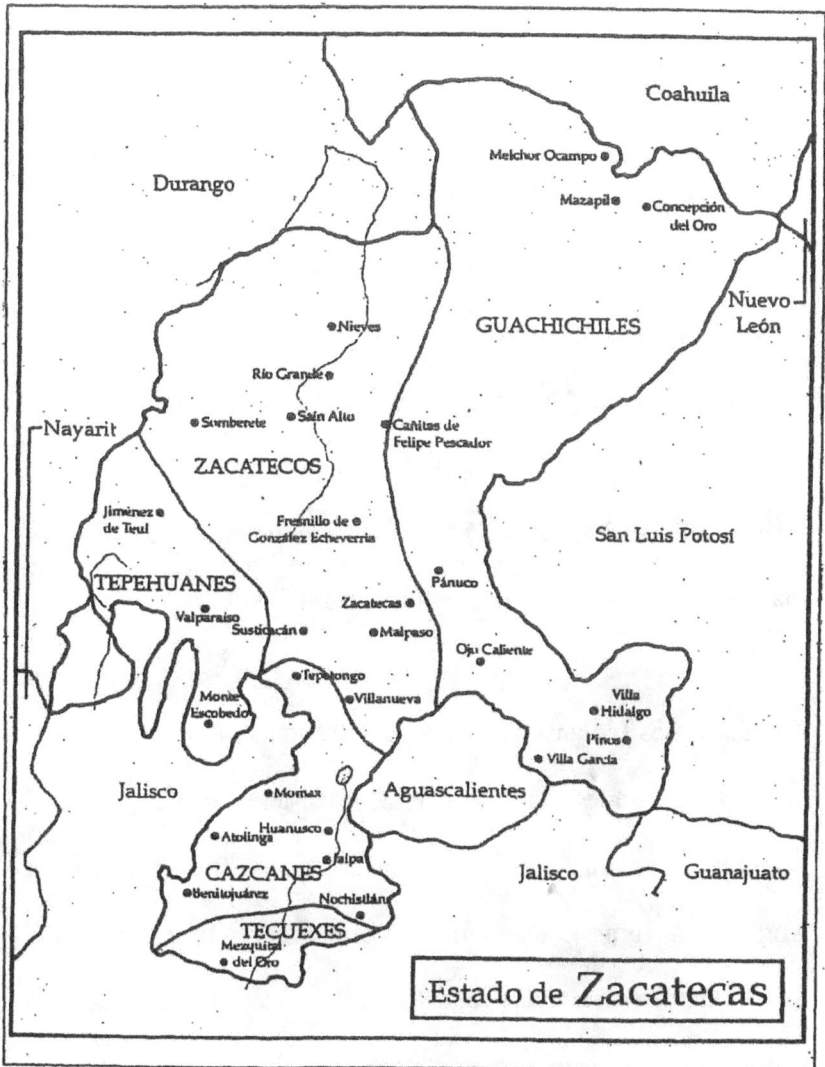

Coahuila

Durango

Melchor Ocampo ●

Mazapil ● ● Concepción
del Oro

Nieves ●

GUACHICHILES

Nuevo
León

Río Grande ●

● Sombrerete ● Sain Alto ● Cañitas de
Felipe Pescador

Nayarit

ZACATECOS

Jiménez ●
de Teul

Fresnillo de ●
González Echeverría

San Luis Potosí

TEPEHUANES

Pánuco ●

Valparaíso
Sustiacán ●

Zacatecas ●
● Malpaso

Oju Caliente ●

● Tepetongo

Monte
Escobedo ●

● Villanueva

Villa
● Hidalgo

Pinos ●
● Villa García

Jalisco

● Momax

Aguascalientes

Huanusco ●
● Atolinga

CAZCANES

● Jalpa

Jalisco

Guanajuato

● Benito Juárez

Nochistlán

TECUEXES

Mezquital
● del Oro

Estado de Zacatecas

The Indigenous Tribes of Zacatecas

ZACATECAS: A DEFIANT LAND

The Zacatecos

The Zacatecos Indians who occupied much of what is now northern Zacatecas and northeastern Durango, lived closest to the silver mines that the Spaniards discovered in 1546. They were also the primary indigenous group occupying the present-day municipio of Sain Alto, where the Dominguez family lived. The lands of the Zacatecos Indians bordered with those of the Tepehuanes on the west and the Guachichiles on the east. They roamed as far north as Parras in present-day Coahuila.

The Zacatecos Indians, occupying 60,000 square kilometers in the present-day states of Zacatecas, eastern Durango, and Aguascalientes, may have received their name from the Mexica word *zacate* (grass). But some contemporary sources have said that the name was actually taken from the Zacatecos language and that it meant *cabeza negra* ("black head").[8] This would be a

---

[8] Philip Wayne Powell, *op. cit.*, p. 237.

reference to the Chichimecas' penchant for painting their bodies and faces with various pigments (in this case, black pigment).

The Zacatecos were "a tall, well-proportioned, muscular people, their strength being evidenced by the great burdens they carried for the Spaniards." They had oval faces with "long black eyes wide apart, large mouth, thick lips and small flat noses." The men wore breechcloth, while the women wore short petticoats of skins or woven maguey. Both sexes wore their hair long, usually to the waist. The Zacatecos married young, with most girls being married by the age of fifteen. Monogamy was their general practice. The Indians smeared their bodies with clay of various colors and painted them with the forms of reptiles. This paint helped shield them from the sun's rays but also kept vermin off their skin.[9]

---

[9] Peter Masten Dunne, *Pioneer Jesuits in Northern Mexico* (Berkeley: University of California Press, 1944), p. 21; J. Lloyd Mecham, *op. cit.*, pp. 62-63; Paul Kirchhoff, "The Hunting-Gathering People of North Mexico," in Basil C. Hedrick et al. (ed.), *The North Mexican Frontier: Readings in Archaeology, Ethnohistory, and Ethnography* (Carbondale, Illinois: Southern Illinois University Press, 1971), p. 204.

ZACATECAS: A DEFIANT LAND

The Zacatecos Indians grew roots, herbs, maize, beans, and some wild fruits. They hunted rabbits, deer, birds, frogs, snakes, worms, moles, rats, and reptiles. Eventually, the Zacatecos and some of the other Chichimecas would develop a fondness for the meat of the larger animals brought in by the Spaniards. During their raids on Spanish settlements, they frequently stole mules, horses, cattle, and other livestock, all of which became a part of their diet.

The Guachichile Indians.

The Guachichiles, of all the Chichimeca Indians, occupied the most extensive territory. Considered both warlike and brave, the Guachichiles roamed through a large section of the present-day state of Zacatecas. Their territory did not include Sain Alto but they did occupy and travel through the regions slightly to the east of Sain Alto.

ZACATECAS: A DEFIANT LAND

The name of "Guachichile" that the Christian Indians gave them meant "heads painted of red," a reference to the red dye that they used to pain their bodies, faces and hair.[10] Although the main home of the Guachichile Indians lay in Zacatecas, they also occupied significant portions of western San Luis Potosí, eastern Aguascalientes, northeastern Jalisco, and southern Coahuila.

In the development of tribal alliances, the Guachichiles were considered the most advanced of the Chichimec tribes. They were a major catalyst in provoking the other tribes to resist the Spanish settlement and exploitation of Indian lands. "Their strategic position in relation to Spanish mines and highways," wrote Dr. Powell, "made them especially effective in raiding and in escape from Spanish reprisal." It was thus very easy for the Guachichiles to disappear quickly into their native lands, where the Spanish soldiers would be reluctant to follow.

---

[10] Philip Wayne Powell, *op. cit.* p. 35; Paul Kirchhoff, *op. cit.*, p. 204.

ZACATECAS: A DEFIANT LAND

The Spanish frontiersmen and contemporary writers referred to the Guachichiles "as being the most ferocious, the most valiant, and the most elusive (or nomadic) of all the Chichimecas." The Christian missionaries found their language difficult to learn because of its "many sharply variant dialects." As a result, the conversion of these natives to Christianity did not come easy.

The Chichimeca War

The author Philip Wayne Powell wrote that "the rush to Zacatecas left in its wake a long stretch of unsettled and unexplored territory." The small mining camps adjacent to the silver mines represented "an isolated nucleus of Spanish settlement in a surrounding vastness of unknown lands and peoples."[11]

As these settlements and the mineral output of the mines grew in numbers, "the needs to transport to and from it became a vital concern of miners, merchants, and government." To function

---

[11] Philip Wayne Powell, *op. cit.*, pp. 14-15.

properly, the Zacatecas silver mines "required well-defined and easily traveled routes." These routes brought in badly needed supplies and equipment from distant towns and also delivered the silver to smelters and royal counting houses in the south.[12]

The strategic location of the Zacatecas mines made confrontation with the Chichimec Indians inevitable. Although Tolosa and other administrators attempted to preserve peaceful relations with the local Indians, early indications of antagonistic intent soon became evident. The demographer Peter Gerhard writes that "the rush of treasure-seekers and the opening of cart-roads from central Mexico to these mines" led to a "displacement of desert tribes" that brought on "a fierce struggle (the Chichimec war) that kept the northern frontier aflame from sea to sea for four decades (1550-1590)."[13]

---

[12] *Ibid.*

[13] Peter Gerhard, *The North Frontier of New Spain* (Princeton: Princeton University Press, 1982), p. 6.

ZACATECAS: A DEFIANT LAND

Dr. Powell wrote that "the highways... became the tangible, most frequently visible evidence of the white man's permanent intrusion in the land of the Chichimecas." This increasingly heavy traffic on the highways attracted the attention of the Chichimecs. As the settlements expanded and new roads were paved, the traffic on these highways came into the view of more tribes. As the natives learned about the usefulness of the goods being transported (silver, food, and clothing), "they quickly appreciated the vulnerability of this highway movement to any attack they might launch."[14]

Thus, the stage was set for the Chichimec War. In 1550, the first strikes were made by Zacatecos Indians who attacked caravans south of the town of Zacatecas. But, soon after, the Guachichiles farther south made even more destructive attacks on the new roads through the Guanajuato Sierras. It is believed that about 120 people were killed in the first months of the war.

---

[14] Philip Wayne Powell, *op. cit.*, p. 16.

ZACATECAS: A DEFIANT LAND

Pacification and Peace

The intensity of the Chichimec War increased over the years, and by 1585, it had reached a climax and official reports stated that highway travel beyond the city of Zacatecas to the more northern mines was all but nonexistent during this time.[15]   However, on October 18, 1585, Alonso Manrique de Zuñiga, the Marqués de Villamanrique, became the seventh viceroy of Mexico. Dr. Powell writes that "to this great viceroy must go the major share of credit for planning and largely effecting the end" of the war and "the development of basic policies to guarantee a sound pacification of the northern frontier." He evaluated the deteriorating situation, consulted expert advice, and reversed the practices of the past.[16]

---

[15] *Ibid.*, pp. 60-63, 172-181; Martha Menchaca, *op. cit.*, p. 77.

[16] Charlotte M. Gradie. *The Tepehuan Revolt of 1616: Militarism, Evangelism, and Colonialism in Seventeenth-Century Nueva Vizcaya* (Salt Lake City: The University of Utah Press, 2000), pp. 46-49; Philip Wayne Powell, *op. cit.*, pp. 183-184.

ZACATECAS: A DEFIANT LAND

After analyzing the situation in Zacatecas, Villamanrique launched a full-scale peace offensive. He opened negotiations with the principal Chichimeca leaders, and, according to Dr. Powell, made to them promises of food, clothing, lands, religious administration, and agricultural implements to attract them to peaceful settlement." As it turns out, the olive branch proved to be more persuasive than the sword, and on November 25, 1589, the Viceroy was able to report to the King that the state of war had ended.

The policy of peace by persuasion was continued under the next Viceroy, Luis de Velasco. He sent Franciscan and Jesuit missionaries into the former war zone and spent more money on food and agricultural tools for the Chichimecas. He also recruited some 400 families of Tlaxcalans from the south and settled them in eight towns of the war zone. Velasco's successor, the Conde de Monterrey, completed Velasco's work by establishing a language school at Zacatecas to teach missionaries the various Chichimeca

32

dialects. Through this effort, the conversion of the Chichimeca Indians to Christianity would be streamlined.

The missionaries became important diplomats of peace during this period. Having learned the native tongues, many of the friars were able to communicate with the Chichimecs in their own language. While the Franciscans were the primary peacemakers and spiritual ministers in most areas of the Gran Chichimeca, the Augustinians became active among the Pames of the eastern Sierra Mountains in Guanajuato. Under Viceroy Velasco, the Jesuits became a more important element of the missionary offensive in the war area.

The Chichimeca War and its aftermath led directly to the cultural extinction and assimilation of the Zacatecos and Guachichile Indians. As the war raged on, the Spaniards relied heavily upon their Indian allies in many ways. According to Dr. Powell, the friendly "Indians formed the bulk of the fighting forces against the

Chichimeca warriors." Elaborating on this issue, Dr. Powell wrote:[17]

> As fighters, as burden bearers, as interpreters, as scouts, as emissaries, the pacified natives of New Spain played significant and often indispensable roles in subjugating and civilizing the Chichimeca country. Occasionally armies composed exclusively of these native warriors (particularly the Otomíes) roamed the tierra de guerra to seek out, defeat, and help Christianize the hostile nomad of the north. On some parts of the frontier defense against Chichimeca attacks was at times exclusively in the hands of the native population...
>
> Spanish authority and personnel were in most cases supervising agents for manpower supplied by Indian allies. The white men were the organizers of the effort; native allies did much of the hard work and often bore the brunt of the fighting. In the early years of the war the Spaniards placed heavy reliance upon those natives who had been wholly or partly subdued by the Cortesian conquest – Mexicans, Tarascans, Otomíes, among others.
>
> This use of native allies... led eventually to a virtual disappearance of the nomadic tribes as they were absorbed into the northward-moving Tarascans, Aztecs, Cholultecans, Otomíes, Tlaxcalans, Cazcanes, and others...

---

[17] *Ibid.* pp. 158-159.

"Within a few decades of the general pacification at the end of the century," explains Dr. Powell, "the Guachichiles, Zacatecos, Guamares, and other tribes or nations were disappearing as distinguishable entities in the Gran Chichimeca."[18]

With these events taking place, my Zacatecos and Guachichile ancestors in Zacatecas rapidly lost their identities as individual ethnic groups, and, as Dr. Powell concluded, "the sixteenth-century land of war thus became fully Mexican in its mixture." And – through this process – my ancestors evolved from fierce Indian warriors into peaceful subjects of the Spanish King.

---

[18] *Ibid.*, p. 59.

A LAND OF TURMOIL

The Struggle for Independence.

Spain ruled over its prize colony of Mexico for three centuries. However, eventually the people of Mexico came to the conclusion that they would prefer to govern themselves. Mexico's War of Independence against Spain began early on the morning of September 16, 1810 when Father Miguel Hidalgo y Costilla (1753-1811) summoned the largely Indian and mestizo congregation of his small Dolores parish church in Guanajuato and urged them to take up arms and fight for Mexico's independence from Spain. His *Grito de Dolores (Cry of Dolores)* maintained the equality of all races and called for redistribution of land.

Within days, a motley band of poorly armed Indians and mestizos made their way to San Miguel, enlisting hundreds of recruits along the way. San Miguel fell to the rebel forces, but when Hidalgo's forces reached the city of Guanajuato on September 28, they met with stiff resistance from royalist forces. Before the day was over, a fierce battle had cost the lives of 500 Spaniards and 2,200

Indians. But the rebels had captured the city and in October, they moved on to take Zacatecas, San Luis Potosí, and Valladolid.

By October, Hidalgo, with a revolutionary army now numbering 80,000 men, approached Mexico City. Although his army defeated a small, well-equipped Spanish army outside of the city, Hidalgo – short on ammunition – ordered a northward retreat. From this point, the Spanish forces began a campaign to recapture lost territory. In March 1811, Hidalgo and other rebel leaders were captured in Coahuila. Most of the rebel leaders were executed as traitors. Found guilty of heresy and treason, Father Hidalgo was executed on July 31st.

The revolutionary cause was next taken up by Father José María Morelos y Pavón (1765-1815). By the spring of 1813, Morelos' rebel army had encircled Mexico City and isolated the capital from both coasts. However, within six months, the Spanish military was able to break the siege and recapture lost territory once again.

A LAND OF TURMOIL

In the fall of 1815, Morelos was captured and executed by a firing squad. With his execution, the Independence movement reached its nadir.

Over the next five years, some sporadic guerilla warfare continued to plague the Spanish military. However, the Mexican Independence movement would receive unexpected help from a foreign ally. In 1820, a revolt of the Spanish military in Spain brought about a renewed vitality on the part of the Mexican people. In December of 1820, a royalist officer, Agustín de Iturbide (1783-1824), switched allegiance and made common cause with the rebel movement.

On February 24, 1821, Agustín de Iturbide declared the Plan of Iguala, calling for an independent, constitutional monarchy headed by an emperor. He entered Mexico City on September 27, 1821, and took power soon after. The Treaty of Córdoba was signed by Agustín de Iturbide and the Spanish viceroy, on August 24, 1821.

This treaty recognized Mexico's independence. However, on May 19, 1822, the Congress named Iturbide as the constitutional emperor of Mexico. Mexico now moved from an absolute monarchy to a constitutional monarch. Within a year, however, Iturbide would be overthrown and Mexico would become a Republic.

According to Dr. Martha Menchaca, the author of *Recovering History, Constructing Race: The Indian, Black, and White Roots of Mexican Americans*, the end of the Revolution brought with it the reality of the devastation wrought by war:[1]

> The war of independence had disastrous effects on the national economy. During the war, fields were destroyed and agricultural production declined, leaving the country in a crisis. There was insufficient food to feed the masses. In the mining industry production practically came to a halt, as many workers had left the mines to join the war and machinery had been damaged. This produced a financial strain, because the mining industry had been one of Mexico's strongest assets, generating

---

[1] Martha Menchaca, *op. cit.*, p. 162.

employment for a large segment of the population...
Mexico also experienced an economic drain when
Spanish elites left the country, taking their assets;
worst of all, the Spanish crown left the Mexican
government bankrupt...

Statehood

On July 12, 1823, Zacatecas declared itself an independent state

within the Mexican Republic. In the years to follow, many of the

Mexican states, including Zacatecas, would seek provincial self-

government and political autonomy from Mexico City. However,

the self-determination that Zacatecas sought for itself came into

direct conflict with the policies of General Antonio López de

Santa Anna Pérez de Lebrón

Many historians have referred to the years from 1823 to 1855 as

the age of Santa Anna. During this period, General Santa Anna

would serve nine terms as President of the Mexican Republic. In

early 1835, when Francisco García, the Governor of Zacatecas,

challenged the authority of the central government, General Santa

Anna marched against him. On May 11, 1835, near the town of Guadalupe, General Santa Anna's federal forces defeated the Zacatecas militia in a two-hour battle. Soon after this victory, Santa Anna's forces ransacked the city of Zacatecas and the rich silver mines at Fresnillo. In addition to seizing large quantities of Zacatecas silver, Santa Anna decided to punish Zacatecas by separating Aguascalientes from Zacatecas and making it into an independent territory.[2]

Benito Juárez

Known as the "Glorious Son of the Americas," Benito Pablo Juárez García (1806-1872), the son of Zapotec Indians from Oaxaca, assumed the presidency of Mexico on January 19, 1858 after the resignation of President Ignacio Comonfort. Given the rules for succession, Juárez, as the President of the Supreme Court of Justice, was next in line for the office of President. Ultimately, he would serve five consecutive terms that ran from 1858 to 1872.

---

[2] The territory of Aguascalientes was granted statehood in 1857.

A LAND OF TURMOIL

However, when the liberal-minded Juárez became president, many of the country's conservatives did not recognize his constitutional mandate. Within days, a military coup by the Conservatives led to the installation of a military officer, General Félix Zuloaga (1813-1898) as President. General Zuloaga started his government under two strict principles: religion and patriotism.

As a result of this rivalry between Mexican conservatives and Mexican liberals, a bitter and bloody confrontation known as the "War of the Reform" (1858-1861) started. Also known as the "Three Year War," this civil war devastated Mexico's already fragile economy. While mining virtually came to a halt, agricultural production declined dramatically.

The War of the Reform was fought in many states, and Zacatecas, unfortunately, was not able to escape the ensuing devastation. During 1858, control of the city of Zacatecas alternated between the opposing armies. On April 19, Conservative troops entered the city, but a week later, Liberal forces – moving south from Nuevo León – recaptured the capital. However, in October, shortly after the Liberal politician Jesús González Ortega became Governor of the state, Conservative forces once again occupied Zacatecas. By the end of January 1859, however, Liberal forces reoccupied the City of Zacatecas.[3]

Early in the war, President Juárez had been forced to flee the county but in 1859 made his way into the port of Veracruz where he set up his administration. It was from Veracruz that Juárez issued the Reform Laws that established the separation between church and state. Through these laws, the nationalization of church property and secularization of cemeteries took place. Juárez also instituted freedom of religion and reduced the number of officially sanctioned religious holidays. The Reform Laws also

---

[3] Ivie E. Cadenhead, *Jesús González Ortega and Mexican National Politics* (Fort Worth: the Texas Christian University Press, 1972) – Texas Christian University Monographs in History and Culture, No. 9, pp. 22-23.

created the Civil Registry Office, which, henceforth, would record marriages and births in each municipio of Mexico.

In 1860 the Liberals gained the upper hand in the war, after Ignacio Zaragoza and Jesús González Ortega combined their forces to win important victories over the Conservative forces. Suffering from deep divisions within its ranks, the Conservative Government finally fell, and in December 1860, victorious Liberal troops entered Mexico City. Soon after, Juárez was able to return to the capital in victory.[4]

European Intervention

Victory, however, did not bring stability. The War of the Reform had exhausted the Mexican treasury, which was nearly empty. In addition, the war had also inflicted a great deal of damage on the

---

[4] The historian Ivie E. Cadenhead discusses the War of the Reform in great detail on pages 21-44 of his monograph, *Jesús González Ortega and the Mexican National Politics.*

property of European nationals, resulting in the accumulation of outstanding debts to several European nations.

As a result, President Juárez was now faced with a devastated economy and a huge foreign debt, neither of which could be alleviated by the empty treasury. In order to avoid an economic disaster, on July 17, 1861, President Juárez declared a two-year moratorium on payments of the foreign debt. In those days, international law permitted the use of armed forces by creditor nations in such situations, so in October 1861, the chief creditors – Great Britain, France, and Spain – protested to Juarez and signed the Convention of London, by which they agreed on a joint occupation of the port of Veracruz to enforce their claims.

The three powers proceeded with a joint military intervention, which commenced on December 14, 1861 when a Spanish contingent of 6,000 men arrived at the port of Veracruz. Then, on January 9, 1862, a French squadron of 2,000 marines – along with

A LAND OF TURMOIL

600 *Zouaves* and soldiers of the line – landed in Veracruz. Soon after, 800 British marines joined the occupation.[5]

Spain and Britain, after holding negotiations with Juárez, withdrew their forces. However, the French, informed by the Conservatives that their forces would be welcomed with open arms in Mexico City, continued their occupation of Veracruz and prepared to march inland towards the capital. In the meantime, President Juárez warned the Mexican people that it was time to defend their native land. González Ortega, who had returned to Zacatecas in triumph in November 1861 – quickly assembled an army of 5,000 to defend the state against the European intrusion.[6]

Cinco de Mayo

On April 19, 1862, 6,000 seasoned French troops under General Charles Laurencz began their march inland towards Mexico City.

---

[5] Ivie E. Cadenhead, *op. cit.*, p. 66.

[6] *Ibid.*, p. 67.

A LAND OF TURMOIL

On May 4, the French forces camped on a plateau close to the city of Puebla, approximately halfway between the Gulf Coast and Mexico City. The next day, General Ignacio Zaragoza, commanding the Mexican forces, decided to attack the French army, hoping to cripple or slow their advance in order to give precious time to the Mexican army in the capital.

The Mexican soldiers, lacking battlefield experience and armed with outdated artillery and muskets, attacked with great determination and fervor. In a four-hour battle, the Mexicans suffered only 250 casualties, while inflicting heavy losses on the French. Losing nearly a thousand men, the French withdrew back to the Gulf Coast to await reinforcements from Europe. Although they were stunned by the disaster at Puebla, the French began to prepare for a new offensive against Mexico City. The Mexican people had won an important battle, but the war was far from finished.

FOUNDING FATHER

Aniceto Dominguez

Into the turmoil and uncertainty of these times was born the man who would become the patriarch and the founder of the Dominguez family in Kansas City. At 8:a.m. on April 22, 1862, as the French moved their forces inland from Veracruz, a 22-year-old laborer named Marcelino Dominguez appeared before the Judge of the Civil Court in Sain Alto to report that his son, Aniceto Dominguez, had been born five days earlier in the Hacienda de Santa Monica. According to the birth record in the Civil Registry office of the municipio of Sain Alto, Aniceto's mother was 19-year-old Petra Salas, the wife of Marcelino Dominguez.

Forty-seven years later, this poor Mexican citizen would forever alter the destiny of his family by bringing his children and grandchildren across the Mexican border into the United States, first to the Texas Panhandle and then to Kansas City.

FOUNDING FATHER

In his life, Aniceto Dominguez would see great technological advances, including the invention of the telephone, the airplane, and the gas-driven automobile. However, Aniceto would also live to see his adopted country take part in two terrible and devastating world wars. In the Second World War, he watched as two of his American-born grandsons marched off to war to defend their native soil. With both pride and sorrow, Aniceto watched as one grandson was killed in action and another was captured by the enemy. By the time he died on October 9, 1946 at the age of 84 years, five months, and 24 days, Aniceto Dominguez had seven grandchildren, 27 great-grandchildren and two great great grandchildren.

The map on the following page shows the northwestern region of Zacatecas, including the towns of Sain Alto and Santa Monica (directly east of Sain Alto and adjacent to Sain Bajo).

González Ortega . Nieves •

Ignacio Zaragoza

El Fuerte o

Ciudad de
Río Grande

Cañas o

Sombrerete

SAIN ALTO

Sain Bajo
Santa Monica

• Mesilla

Río de Medina

Corrales

Altamira

El Barranco

Fresnillo

North

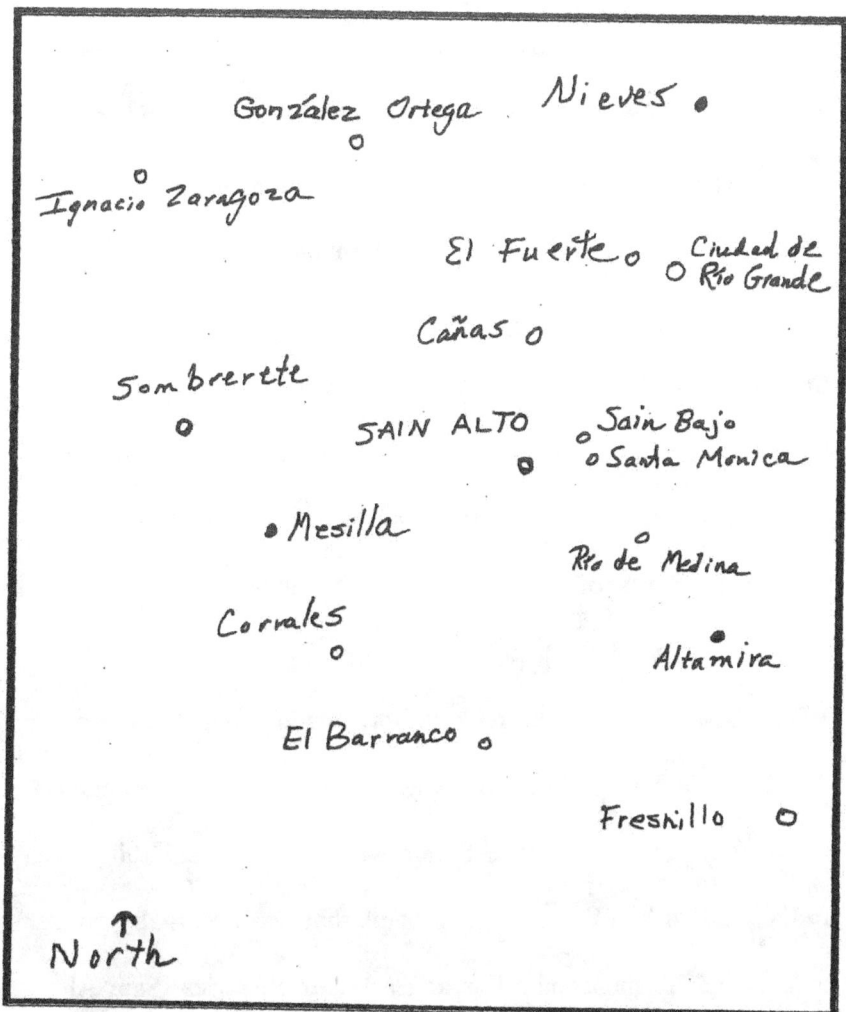

Northwestern Zacatecas

51

FOUNDING FATHER

The Municipio of Sain Alto

The city of Sain Alto – located 128 kilometers (98 miles) northwest of the city of Zacatecas – was established in 1554 by Francisco de Ibarra. The Zacatecos Indians were the primary indigenous group living in the area of Sain Alto at the time of the Spanish contact, although Guachichiles and Tecuexes may have lived in the area. Spanish explorers first passed through the area in 1552, and in 1555, the silver mines at San Martín – a short distance northwest of Sombrerete – were founded.

When Ibarra left Sain Alto for new horizons in 1554, he left Señor Fernando Sain in charge of the nearby Chacuaco mine and its surrounding area. Because Señor Sain was tall and thin, the Indians called him "Sain Alto," a name that was eventually given to the land he managed. For at least four centuries, Sain Alto existed in the shadow of her larger better-known neighbor, Sombrerete, which is about forty-five miles west of Sain Alto.

FOUNDING FATHER

Sombrerete was founded on June 6, 1555 by a group of Spaniards and Indians from the south. The town was named for a nearby hill, whose shape resembled that of a sombrero. The area surrounding both Sombrerete and Sain Alto was under constant attack by Chichimec warriors during these early years, but by 1590, the hostilities had ended. By this time, Spanish settlers in Sain Alto had established cattle ranches and wheat farms, with Tlaxcalans, Zacatecos and Africans supplying most of the labor.[1]

When rich silver ores were discovered near Sombrerete in 1646, the ensuing mining boom brought a new surge of entrepreneurs and laborers into the general area. During this period, Sain Alto became a Spanish presidio. However, according to Peter Gerhard, Sain Alto was later made into "an ore-processing and stock-raising center" and was considered a "predominantly Indian settlement" surrounded by many ranchos and haciendas.[2] For most of the

---

[1] Peter Gerhard, *op. cit.*, p. 131.

[2] *Ibid.*, pp. 132.

colonial period, Sain Alto served as a subordinate community to its larger neighbor, Sombrerete. However, in 1824, Sain Alto was promoted to the status of municipio within the newly independent Mexican Republic.

San Sebastián Church in Sain Alto was founded in 1790 and was named for the Christian martyr Saint Sebastian who was killed in Rome during the Third Century A.D. Sebastian, whose feast day is celebrated on January 20, is considered the patron saint of archers and soldiers. Each year from January 17th to the 20th, the parishioners of Sain Alto hold a traditional festival in which they perform the Danza de las Palmas (Dance of the Palms) to signify the first encounter of the Aztec Emperor Moctezuma with Hernán Cortés.

No histories have been written for the city of Sain Alto, but the local people still talk about the time that Pancho Villa's troops arrived at the residence of some Spanish people near the outskirts of town. Villa's troops massacred these foreigners and – to this day – the building that housed the victims is avoided by the townspeople.

According to Zacatecas government statistics, the municipio of Sain Alto had a total population of 21,779 in 1995. This figure represented only 1.63% of the state's entire population. Within the municipio, the capital city of Sain Alto boasted a population of almost 5,000, while the nearby town of Sain Bajo, to which the Hacienda de Santa Monica belonged, had a population of 962. Río de Medina, located in the southeast corner of the municipio, had over 2,000 inhabitants.[3] By the time of the 2000 census, however, the population of the municipio actually dropped to 20,775 individuals.[4]

---

[3] INEGI. *Estados Unidos Mexicanos. Conteo de Población y Vivienda, 1995.*

[4] INEGI. *Resultados Definitivos del XII Censo General de Población y Vivienda.*

FOUNDING FATHER

French Occupation

In the months following the Battle of Puebla, my great great grandparents, Marcelino Dominguez and Petra Salas, were preoccupied with their newborn infant, Aniceto. However, as they dealt with their day-to-day responsibilities in their small community, the leaders of the Mexican Republic tried to anticipate the next move of the French invaders. The French military authorities had greatly overestimated the support that they expected from the Mexican people. Instead of rallying to the cause of the Europeans, the Mexican people were preparing to resist with all the means available to them.

But the French Emperor Napoleon III (1808-1873) had already invested too much in this foreign gamble and was not willing to withdraw his troops from eastern Mexico. Instead, he dispatched another 30,000 French soldiers under the command of General Frederic Forey to Mexico. A year after the Battle of Puebla, the reinforced French forces resumed their march inland towards

Mexico City. Once again, the French marched on the city of Puebla – now renamed Puebla de Zaragoza to honor the recently deceased General Zaragoza.

When the French laid siege to the city on March 21, 1863, they boasted a force of 26,000 soldiers, while the Mexican defenders had 22,000 men under arms. For almost two months, the Mexican army held out against increasing French pressure. On May 17, the siege of Puebla ended and the victorious French forces occupied the city, more than a year after their humiliating defeat on Cinco de Mayo.[5]

It was not long before the French captured Mexico City, where they would install Maximilian of Hapsburg as the Emperor of Mexico in June 1864. Juárez and his government were forced to abandon the capital and established a new government in San Luis Potosí. However, in late 1863, as French forces captured

---

[5] Ivie E. Cadenhead, *op. cit.*, pp. 70-75.

Querétaro, Morelia (Michoacán), San Miguel Allende, Guanajuato, León and Lagos de Moreno, Juárez recognized that the French successes endangered his position in San Luis Potosí. On December 22, 1863, Juárez moved his government north to Saltillo, the capital of Coahuila.[6]

In the meantime, Jesús González Ortega – the steadfast supporter of the Mexican cause in Zacatecas – was forced to abandon the City of Zacatecas in February 1864. He moved first to Fresnillo and then to Sain Alto and Sombrerete as the French advance continued northward. By the early summer, the French controlled large parts of Mexico. However, Mexican rebels operated in many areas of Sinaloa, Sonora, Durango, Chihuahua, Nuevo León and Tamaulipas. In the south, the rebel forces of General Porfirio Díaz occupied large parts of Guerrero, Oaxaca, Tabasco and Chiapas.[7]

---

[6] *Ibid.*, p. 85.

[7] *Ibid.*, pp. 85-87.

FOUNDING FATHER

The French occupation of Mexico would continue until early 1867, during which time Juárez repeatedly moved the site of his government from Chihuahua to Zacatecas and back to San Luis Potosí. By 1867, the French – preoccupied by events in Europe – decided to withdraw their troops and Emperor Maximilian was left without his primary means of support. As the French troops marched back to the port of Veracruz, the Liberal Army gained momentum and captured Guadalajara, Oaxaca, Monterrey, and Tampico. Once the French forces had evacuated Veracruz and returned to France, Emperor Maximilian – lacking any significant military support – was surrounded by Mexican troops and captured on May 15, 1867. Soon after, he was executed.

Fifty thousand Mexicans lost their lives fighting the French forces. But the experience, although tragic and costly, led to the beginning of a national self-esteem that began to grow perceptibly in the years to follow. On July 15, 1867, Benito Juárez returned to Mexico City to resume his post as President of the Republic. He would serve two more terms as President until July 19, 1872 when he died of a coronary seizure. In the meantime, Sain Alto and the state of Zacatecas once more experienced peace. For the next four decades, the Mexican Republic would be at peace with itself and the rest of the world.

A FAMILY OF SILVER MINERS

The Silver Industry

It is believed that most of my Dominguez, Salas and Lujan ancestors from Sain Alto were laborers who worked the nearby silver and mercury mines. My great-great- grandfather Marcelino Dominguez was a miner, and it is believed that his father Manual Dominguez – also a native of Santa Monica – had also been a miner in the early years of the Mexican Republic. It was assumed that Aniceto would follow in the footsteps of his father and grandfather.

After the French were expelled from Mexico in 1867, silver production in the Republic rose rapidly, stimulated by new silver deposit discoveries. Throughout the 1870s production increased at an annual growth rate of over two percent. Under the regime of President Porfirio Díaz – who succeeded Benito Juárez – the silver industry continued to grow and play an important role in the spectacular economic growth of the Republic. In 1877-1878, silver alone accounted for 60 percent of the value of all Mexican exports.[1]

Professor Mark Wasserman explains that "mining led the Porfirian boom. Demand for silver and non-precious metals, such as copper and zinc, in Europe and the United States provided the markets." In the last decades of the Nineteenth Century, the installation of electric power and the introduction of cyanide into the refining process had greatly enhanced profitability in the mining industry. Electricity would provide light, powered pumps, trams, and other crucial equipment. These improvements were able to reduce costs so that old mines were reopened and worked once again.[2]

Miners earned the highest wages in Mexico, but their work was very dangerous. Some miners actually worked part-time in the mines but also maintained property that they cultivated.

---

[1] Mark Wasserman, *op. cit.*, pp. 72, 174.

[2] *Ibid*, pp. 174-175.

A FAMILY OF SILVER MINERS

Throughout the Porfiriato, however, the supervisory and highly skilled jobs went to foreigners. In his work, *Everyday Life and Politics in Nineteenth Century Mexico: Men, Women, and War*, Professor Wasserman, discussing the mining industry in Nineteenth Century Mexico, wrote:[3]

> The work was enormously difficult. In a typical silver mine, workers first dug a short tunnel into a hillside and then excavated straight down. They climbed in and out of the shaft on eight- to ten-foot notched logs. They cut the shafts to follow the veins. Drillers (barreteros) were the top of the underground hierarchy. They earned the highest wages, as much as 3 pesos a day. In the shaft drillers used steel-tipped iron rods to tear loose the ore. Other less skilled workers then hauled 150- to 200-pound bull hide sacks up the log ladders to the surface and emptied the sacks in the dump. If there was no stamp mill, workers crushed the ore and then put it into a trough, where water poured over it. Workers hauled the water. They then sacked the washed ore in 200-pound bags. The mine shipped the bags to the smelter. Workers who hauled ore earned 18 to 20 centavos a day....
>
> The introduction of new machinery, such as pneumatic drills and electric-powered machinery, led

---

[3] *Ibid*, pp. 194-196.

to increased disease and accidents. The change from drilling with a bar and sledge and blasting with black powder to pneumatic drill and dynamite, the use of hoists, and new drainage and ventilation equipment demanded a new kind of worker. Experience, intelligence, and judgment were less important than obedience and diligence. The demand for unskilled labor rose. Unskilled labor (peons) came to comprise two-thirds to three-quarters of the workforce. They were shovelers, rock breakers, ore sorters, car men, and helpers who had come from rural areas. Skilled workers continued to drill the ore, install timber, and operate and maintain machinery...

Mining was a hazardous profession. It is believed that the average life expectancy of a silver miner in Nineteenth Century Mexico was about thirty-seven years. It is thus very reasonable to assume that, if possible, a family might seek to improve its fortune by looking for greener pastures in other professions. From 1877 to 1910, some 300,000 Mexicans – many of them displaced rural workers – settled in northern Mexico. And, according to Professor Wasserman, "the north was for many transient workers only a stopover, for their preferred destination was the United States where employers offered double the pay."[4]

Aniceto and Martina

For the last four decades of the Nineteenth Century, my family lived in the Hacienda de Santa Monica in the municipio of Sain Alto. For generations, various members of my family were engaged in the business of mining silver, gold, and mercury. Aniceto had already worked the mines for several years when he got married at the age of twenty.

Thanks to the Reform Law of July 23, 1859, enacted by the Liberal Party, Aniceto would be married twice, first in a civil ceremony, and secondly, in a church service. The Reform Law had mandated the recording of civil marriages in each municipio of Mexico. So it was that, on April 28, 1882, Aniceto Dominguez and Martina Segovia – both twenty years of age and natives of La

---

[4] *Ibid*, pp. 196-197.

Hacienda de Santa Monica, appeared before the civil magistrate, Francisco Leal, and declared that they were both celibates and desired to be joined in marriage.

Aniceto's mother, Petra Salas had died more than a decade earlier in June 1871, and eight months later, his father Marcelino Dominguez was married to his second wife, 18-year-old María Luisa Salas, a native of San Juan Guadalupe in Durango. By this time, Aniceto had several younger siblings from both Petra and María Salas.

As might be expected in the rural Mexico of this era, Aniceto's wife came from a family that lived and worked on the same hacienda as his family. Martina Segovia was the legitimate daughter of a sixty-year-old laborer Regino Segovia and his wife, Rafaela Alamos. A month after their civil marriage, on May 28,

A FAMILY OF SILVER MINERS

1882, Aniceto and Martina walked down the aisle of San Sebastián Church to take their marriage vows before God.

The parish priest, Father Jacinto Silva had questioned both Aniceto and Martina to determine their readiness for marriage. Certain that there existed no impediments to this marriage, Father Silva issued the marriage banns for Aniceto and Martina on three separate days, a requirement that had been mandated centuries earlier by the Holy Council of Trent (1545-1563).

The newlyweds Aniceto and Martina settled into their married life as another generation of Santa Monica residents. For two years, Aniceto labored in the mines while Martina took care of her household chores. In time, their prayers for a healthy newborn child were answered and Martina became pregnant. Finally, at nine in the morning on October 9, 1884, the twenty-two-year-old laborer, Aniceto Dominguez – accompanied by two friends, Tomas Herrera and Nicolas Martinez – showed up at the office of the civil registrar in Sain Alto to proudly display his infant child, Geronimo Dominguez, who had been born a few days earlier on September 30, 1884.

With Tomas and Nicolas as his witnesses, Aniceto gave the registrar the relevant information about his child's birth. Since the witnesses also lived in La Hacienda de Santa Monica, they helped Aniceto fulfill his civic duty of informing the government about this new citizen of the Mexican Republic.

After reporting the birth of his child and baptizing him in the church, Aniceto and Martina raised little Geronimo in the Hacienda. Although Aniceto and Martina would have more children, Martina eventually died in childbirth and Aniceto was left as a widower with several children to care for.

A FAMILY OF SILVER MINERS

Geronimo and Luisa

At the turn of the century when Geronimo Dominguez turned sixteen, the Dominguez family still lived in La Hacienda of Santa Monica. It was around this time that the young Geronimo took an interest in Luisa Lujan, a teen-aged girl who had also been born and raised in Santa Monica. It seems likely that both Geronimo and Luisa may have attended the small chapel at the hacienda. It is equally likely that Geronimo and Luisa occasionally saw each other at religious festivals at San Sebastián church in Sain Alto.

Finally, at ten in the morning on November 28, 1903, Geronimo Dominguez and Luisa Lujan appeared in the office of Salóme Velasquez, the Judge of the Sain Alto Civil Court, to express their desire to be married. Geronimo was now 19 years old and his young bride, Luisa Lujan, was 17 years old. They informed the Judge that they were both celibates and that they had been born and presently resided in La Hacienda de Santa Monica. By this time, Geronimo had already become a miner. In these early years, he developed a distinctive hacking cough that resulted from his mining activities and would plague him for the rest of his life.

Luisa was the daughter of Urbano Lujan and María Luisa Fraile and the granddaughter of Bonifacio Lujan and Simona Rodriguez. The Lujan family's roots stretched back several generations in La Hacienda de Santa Monica. Like Geronimo, Luisa had been the first-born child of her parents. The 35-year-old laborer Urbano Lujan and 29-year-old María Luisa Fraile had been married in Sain Alto on January 5, 1884, but both of them had been widowed from their previous marriages. María, in fact, first married a Geronimo Lujan, who had the same surname that Urbano had.

Shortly after their marriages in late 1903, both Geronimo and Aniceto appear to have moved their families to Rancho Paso de la Cruz in the southeastern portion of the Sain Alto municipio. Because of the rancho's proximity to the Hacienda de Río de

A FAMILY OF SILVER MINERS

Medina, both Geronimo and Aniceto's families would begin to attend services in the small chapel in that hacienda.

Geronimo and Luisa would not have to wait very long before the birth of their first child. At eight o'clock in the morning of April 2, 1905, Luisa would give birth to my Uncle Pablo at home in Paso de la Cruz. Six days later, on April 8, Geronimo and Luisa brought little Pablo to the chapel at Río de Medina. Father Lucio Huerta greeted them warmly and performed the baptism, pouring Holy Oil and Sacred Chrism over the infant child. Nicolas Medrano and Rosario Natera also attended the small service to take on the responsibility of godparents for little Pablo. Father Huerta looked at the godparents and stressed that their parental and spiritual obligations should be taken very seriously.

Little did Geronimo and Luisa realize that between 1905 and 1926, they would have a total of nine children: Pablo, Felicitas, Jesús María, Raul, Juliana, Pabla (Bessie), Ephifania, Erminio,

Marshall and Louis. All but the first two children would be born as American citizens in either Texas or Kansas. Geronimo and his father Aniceto both realized that Mexico's political and economic condition was experiencing profound changes that would soon cause severe repercussions to Mexican society. "For most Mexicans," writes Professor Mark Wasserman, "the end of the century brought a new kind of misery with its origins in the burgeoning economy based on mineral and agricultural exports. The chasm between wealth and poverty deepened, as the rich grew richer and the poor grew poorer." More and more people started to migrate to the northern mining camps or to railroad centers of the United States in search for employment. As a result, "the process of alienation from the land and, to some extent, from traditional kinship support networks" began.[5]

---

[5] *Ibid*, pp. 183-184.

TRANSPORTATION REVOLUTION

Mexico's Railroad System

In 1877, President Porfirio Díaz decided to initiate the construction of a modern rail network for Mexico. The result of this construction program would be a dramatic increase of the Mexican Republic's railway trackage from 700 miles in 1880 to over 12,000 miles in 1900 and more than 15,000 miles by 1910. In her Doctorate Thesis for the University of California at San Diego, the film director Lorena M. Parlee explained that President Díaz hoped that a continued expansion of the railroad network "would allow the nation to develop its rich natural resources for export, which, in turn, would generate foreign exchange needed for internal investment and government revenue."[1]

Díaz and his supporters also believed that the railroads would provide "easy access to markets" and "would stimulate Mexico's

---

[1] Lorena M. Parlee, *Porfirio Diaz, Railroads, and Development in Northern Mexico: A Study of Government Policy Toward the Central and Nacional Railroads, 1876-1910* (Ann Arbor, Michigan: University Microfilms International, 1981), p. 2.

internal commerce, agriculture, industry and mineral production."
In addition, however, Mexican officials also believed that the rail
lines would allow "the central government to consolidate its
political and economic power over the nation."[2]

And so it was that the Mexican National and the Mexican Central
Railroads were built and soon became and remained major north-
south conduits of people and goods for most of the Twentieth
Century. Both railroads facilitated the opening up of and delivery
to important American markets in the north and a subsequent drop
in transportation costs. The new markets encouraged a significant
growth in commercial agriculture and ranching as well as a
renewal of the mining boom that had maintained Mexico for so
many centuries.

---

[2] *Ibid.*

TRANSPORTATION REVOLUTION

Although Diaz had hoped to attract foreign investment and assert greater control over the northern states of Mexico, his railroad-building program had "an unexpected outcome." The new rail networks made it easier for poor Mexicans to travel long distances from home in search of work. Thus, the railways inadvertently began to draw thousands of Mexican workers steadily northward.[3]

The most important railroad built during these early years was the Mexican Central Railway (*Ferrocarril Central Mexicano*). From 1880 to 1884, an aggressive railroad-building program brought this railroad up the Central Valley of Mexico, providing a direct link between Mexico City and the northern border. By April 1884, this route consisted of 1,969 kilometers (1,224 miles) of rails that ran from Mexico City through Aguascalientes, Zacatecas, and Chihuahua to the border towns of Paso del Norte (now Ciudad

---

[3] Mark Wasserman, *op. cit.*, pp. 171, 184; Juan R. Garcia, *Mexicans in the Midwest, 1900-1932* (Tucson: The University of Arizona Press, 1996), pp. 5-6.

Juárez), Chihuahua and El Paso, Texas.[4] For several decades, this railway was controlled by the mighty Atchison, Topeka, and Santa Fe (ATSF) Railroad, one of the gigantic American corporations that dominated access to the entire western U.S.A.[5] In 1888, Paso del Norte was renamed Ciudad Juárez to honor the late President Benito Juárez.

Ciudad Juárez and the Mexican Central became a crucial link with many parts of the Mexico. Ciudad Juárez lay 1,217 kilometers (756 miles) from Zacatecas, and a total of 1,552 kilometers (964 miles) from Guadalajara (in the state of Jalisco). The distance between Ciudad Juárez and the old colonial city of Guanajuato was 1,493 kilometers (928 miles). The city and state of

[4] The Mexican Central Railway Company Limited, *Facts and Figures About Mexico and Her Great Railroad, The Mexican Central* (Mexico City: Mexican Central Railway Company Limited, 1900 – Third edition), p. 63; John H. McNeely, *The Railways of Mexico: A Study in Nationalization* – Southwestern Studies No. 5 (El Paso: Texas Western Press, 1964), pp. 14-15.

[5] The ATSF is known today as the BNSF (Burlington Northern Santa Fe), following the December 31, 1996 merger of the Santa Fe with the Burlington Northern Railroad Company.

Guanajuato – positioned along this important railway – would be major source of immigrants to the U.S. during the first decades of the Twentieth Century.

Mexico to Texas Railway Connections

Across the border from Ciudad Juárez, El Paso has – for well over a century – been the most important port of entry for northbound migrants from Mexico. For a long time, the people of El Paso, Texas had hoped that the construction of a railroad to their town would bring about a new prosperity. But, in 1877, the nearest railhead was still more than five hundred miles away.[6]

Located in the westernmost part of Texas at the point where the Rio Grande River intersects with the Texas-New Mexico state line, El Paso represented a strategic point between the American railroad network and the central Mexican heartland. In May 1881,

---

[6] Edward A. Leonard, *Rails at the Pass of the North* – Southwestern Studies Monograph No. 63 (El Paso: Texas Western Press, 1981), p. 5.

the Southern Pacific Railroad reached El Paso from Los Angeles. A month later, the Santa Fe Railroad arrived in El Paso from Santa Fe, New Mexico on June 11, 1881. In essence, the Mexican Central Railroad, linking up with the Santa Fe at El Paso/Ciudad Juárez, became an extension of the Santa Fe into Mexico, in large part because it was owned by the same group of Boston financiers who controlled the American company and it was chartered by the state of Massachusetts.[7]

The second major rail route constructed from Mexico City to the northern border was the Mexican National Railway (*Ferrocarriles Nacionales de México*), which was constructed in 1881. Once completed, this railway ran from Mexico City through Saltillo and Monterrey to Nuevo Laredo, Tamaulipas. Across the border from Nuevo Laredo lay the Laredo Port of Entry in Webb County, Texas. The distance from Nuevo Laredo to Zacatecas is about 691 kilometers (429 miles), to Guadalajara it is 1,007 kilometers (626

---

[7] *Ibid.*, p. 30; John H. McNeely, *op. cit.*, pp. 14-15.

miles), and it is 1,187 kilometers (737 miles) from Nuevo Laredo to Mexico City. Initially called the Texas Mexican Railway, this link was constructed in November 1881, but did not come under the control of the National Railroad Company of Mexico until the first years of the Twentieth Century.

"By the turn of the century," explains Ms. Parlee, "the Central and the Nacional [railroads] controlled over half of all railroad track in Mexico and operated the only rail links between Mexico City and the northern border." However, "instead of bringing economic independence, the railroads facilitated the penetration of U.S. capital in other areas of the economy, making Mexico subject to U.S. financial control."[8]

Although, these two railroads "played a crucial role in the development of northern Mexico, stimulating a mining boom and

---

[8] Lorena M. Parlee, *op. cit.*, pp. xii-xiii.

a tremendous growth in commercial agriculture and ranching," Ms. Parlee notes that "the very railroads which the Díaz administration had so strongly promoted to consolidate national unity created strong, regional economic interest groups in northern Mexico, which eventually led to Días' downfall."[9] On the following page, we have reproduced another map from the Department of Commerce *Trade Promotion Series No. 16*, in which the reader can see some of the railroads that connected the interior of Mexico with the Texas border.

One of the most significant links would eventually reach the Eagle Pass port of entry in Maverick County, Texas. Across the border from Eagle Pass is Piedras Negras in the state of Coahuila. In 1883, the *Ferrocarril Internacional Mexicano* (International Mexican Railroad) reached Piedras Negras.

---

[9] *Ibid.*, pp. xii, xiv.

Railroads to the Texas-Mexico Border, 1925

In 1908, however, this line was taken over by the *Ferrocarriles Nacionales de México.*[10] The Piedras Negras connection was an important conduit for travelers making their way from the states of San Luis Potosí, Nuevo León, Coahuila, Zacatecas, and Central Mexico. In many ways, the Piedras Negras-Eagle Pass connection represented a more convenient departure point than El Paso for Mexican nationals going to Houston and other eastern Texas cities.

The distance from Piedras Negras to Monterrey, Nuevo León is 413 kilometers (257 miles) and from Piedras Negras to the City of San Luis Potosi it is 950 kilometers (590 miles). Anyone making the journey from Piedras Negras to Zacatecas will probably travel about 874 kilometers (543 miles). The distance to Guadalajara in the state of Jalisco amounts to a journey of 1,190 kilometers (739

---

[10] "MEXLIST: The Mexican List for Railroad Information: USA - Mexico railroad gateways and related trackage," http://mexican.railspot.com/minsk3.htm. Updated January 12, 2003. Accessed June 8, 2003.

miles). Piedras Negras' crucial link to the Mexican capital represented a distance of 1302 kilometers (809 miles).

The Brownsville Port of Entry sits on the Rio Grande River a few miles west of the Gulf of Mexico and across from the city of Matamoros, Tamaulipas. Brownsville, as the largest city in the lower Rio Grande Valley, is 438 kilometers (272 miles) from San Antonio, Texas and 566 kilometers (352 miles) from Houston, and 832 kilometers (517 miles) from Dallas.

The *Ferrocarril Nacional Mexicano* (Mexican National Railroad) reached Matamoros in 1883 and provided that city with an important link to the Mexican interior. In the Twentieth Century, this railroad would link up with the St. Louis, Brownsville, and Mexico Railroad, which proceeded northward into the interior of Texas. The City of Matamoros came to represent an important link for eastern Mexico with Texas. The distance between Matamoros and the capital of Tamaulipas, Ciudad Victoria, is 312 kilometers (194 miles). The distance between Matamoros and the port city of Veracruz is 916 kilometers (569 miles).

Mexico to Arizona Railway Connections

The Douglas, Arizona port of entry is located in southeastern Cochise County, 351 kilometers (218 miles) west of El Paso, Texas and 189 kilometers (118 miles) southeast of Tucson. It is also 368 kilometers (229 miles) to Phoenix, Arizona. The sister city of Douglas is Agua Prieta in the state of Sonora. Agua Prieta came to represent an important link for American mining interests in the Sonora area. The *Compañia del Ferrocarril de Nacozari*, which was owned by the El Paso & Southwestern Railroad, reached Agua Prieta in 1901.[11]

In the central zone, the development of extensive rail routes from central Mexico to the western American border was a slower

---

[11] "MEXLIST: The Mexican List for Railroad Information: USA - Mexico railroad gateways and related trackage," http://mexican.railspot.com/minsk2.htm. Updated January 12, 2003. Accessed June 8, 2003.

process. Although some railroads connected American business interests in Arizona with the mineral resources of the state of Sonora, passenger service was limited at first. On the following page, the reader will see another map from the Department of Commerce *Trade Promotion Series No. 16*, showing the Sonora and Chihuahua rail links to Arizona and Texas in 1925.

Nogales is the principal city and county seat of Santa Cruz County, the smallest and southernmost of Arizona's counties. The first American railroad arrived in Nogales in 1882. The sister city of Nogales, Arizona is Nogales, Sonora, which also received its first rail link from the south in 1882. In that year, the *Compañia Limitada del Ferrocarril de Sonora*, owned by the Atchison, Topeka & Santa Fe Railway, reached the Mexican Nogales. Initially, Nogales was not an important link to Mexico proper because it had no direct access to Mexico City or to Guadalajara (Mexico's second largest city).

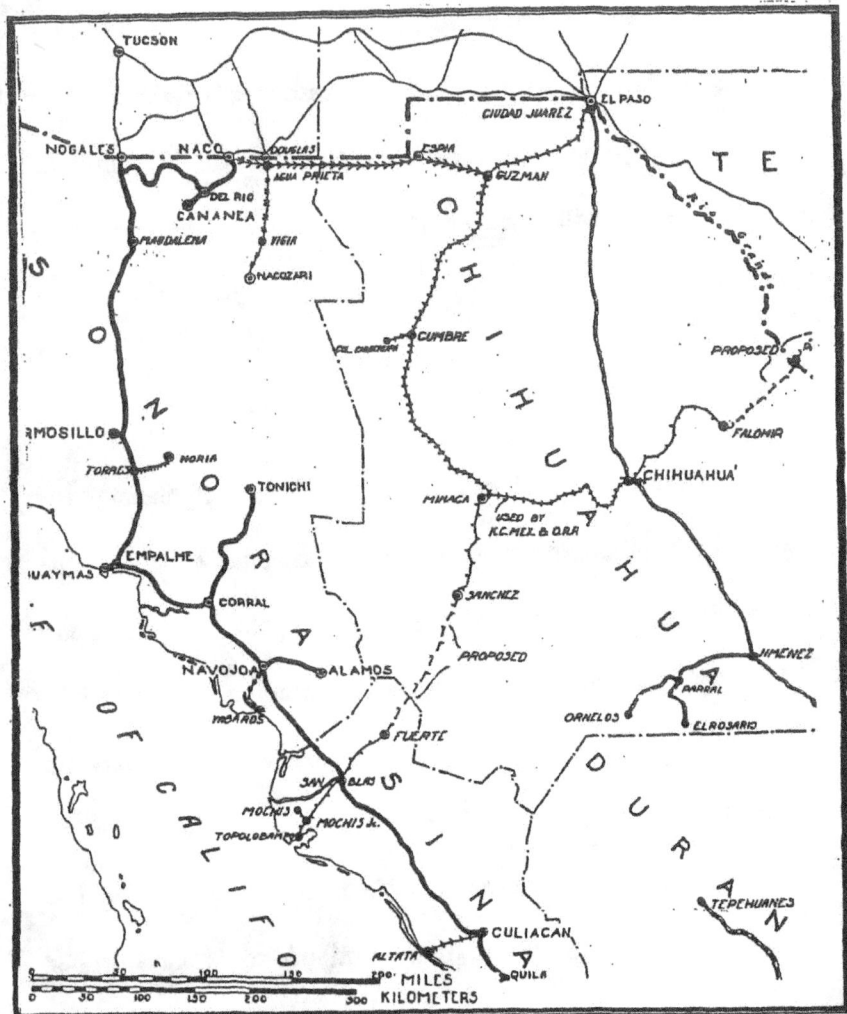

Mexican Rail Links to Arizona and Texas, 1925

TRANSPORTATION REVOLUTION

Then, in April 1927, with the completion of the Southern Pacific of Mexico Railroad linking Guadalajara with Nogales, Arizona, the dynamics of the northward migration were changed significantly. Up until 1927, existing railway lines had forced most immigrants from Guadalajara and the populous state of Jalisco to enter the U.S. by way of El Paso. Now, however, an immediate influx of immigrants from Jalisco were able to make their way north to work in California and Arizona via Nogales.[12] The distance between Nogales and Guadalajara is 1,697 kilometers (1,055 miles), while the distance from Nogales, Sonora to Mexico City is 2,277 kilometers (1,414 miles).

The railroad network of Mexico became an indispensable factor in the massive migration of Mexican laborers to American markets

---

[12] Mark Reisler, *By the Sweat of Their Brow: Mexican Immigrant Labor in the United States, 1900-1940* (Westport, Connecticut: Greenwood Press, 1976), p. 26; "New S.P. de M.R.R. Open to Traffic," *Nogales International*, April 17, 1927; John P. Schmal and Donna S. Morales, *Mexican-American Genealogical Research: Following the Paper Trail to Mexico"* (Bowie, Maryland: Heritage Books, Inc., 2002), p. 71.

during the Twentieth Century. It is not likely that President Díaz and his advisers foresaw that the network would draw such large numbers of Mexicans away from their homes and lead to a dramatic increase in the Mexican-American population of their northern neighbor.

MEXICAN IMMIGRATION, 1848-1930

Mexican Americans in the Nineteenth Century

The immigration of Mexicans to the United States is not a new phenomenon. A large portion of the southwestern U.S.A. had belonged to Mexico up until the Mexican-American War of 1846-1847. But, with the signing of the Treaty of Guadalupe Hidalgo on February 2, 1848, the United States extended its frontier to the Pacific Ocean and received more than 525,000 square miles of Mexican territory that included the present-day states of Arizona, California, western Colorado, Nevada, New Mexico, Texas, and Utah.

At the time of the Treaty, an estimated 82,500 Mexican citizens inhabited the states, which the United States was occupying. Sixty thousand of this number resided in New Mexico, while 14,000 lived in Texas and another 7,500 lived in California. A mere thousand individuals living in Arizona were Mexican citizens. All but two thousand of the 82,500 persons chose to accept their new status as American citizens.   Seven percent of today's Mexican-Americans are believed to be descended from this core group.

The early influx of Anglo-Americans altered the demographics of these American acquisitions and, by 1850, Mexicans in Texas and California represented only ten percent of the two states' total populations. During the second half of the Nineteenth Century, a small but steady stream of Mexican labor continued to travel north. In 1880, 68,399 persons tallied in the Federal Census stated that Mexico was their place of birth. The vast majority of these lived in four southwestern states: Arizona (9,330 persons), California (8,648), New Mexico (5,173) and Texas (43,161). The number of Mexican natives tallied in the 1890 census was 77,853.[1]

---

[1] U.S. Bureau of the Census, *Historical Statistics of the United States, Colonial Times to 1957: A Statistical Abstract Supplement* (Washington, D.C.: U.S. Government Printing Office, 1960), p. 66.

MEXICAN IMMIGRATION, 1848-1930

Immigration after 1900

In the 1900 Federal Census, the number of Mexican-born residents tallied in the United States reached 103,393. But eighty percent of this number was living in Texas and Arizona. The estimated number of ethnic Mexicans living in Texas was 70,000 – representing less than three percent of a total population of more than three million. The number of ethnic Mexicans living in Arizona in 1900 was 14,172, which represented less than 12 percent of the total population of that state. In California, only 8,086 Mexican-born persons were counted in a total population of 1,485,053. However, this figure did not include the descendants of Mexicans who had been living in California for a half a century or more. New Mexico's Mexican-born population of 6,649 represented less than four percent of the total state population of 195,310.[2]

---

[2] George J. Sánchez, *Becoming Mexican American: Ethnicity, Culture, and Identity in Chicano Los Angeles, 1900 - 1945* (New York: Oxford University Press, 1993), pp. 18-19; Arthur F. Corwin, "Early Mexican Labor Migration: A Frontier Sketch, 1848-1900," in *Immigrants – and Immigrants: Perspectives on Mexican Labor Migration to the United States*, Arthur F. Corwin, ed., (Westport, Conn.: Greenwood, 1979), pp. 25-37.

MEXICAN IMMIGRATION, 1848-1930

Between 1820 and 1900, the average annual number of Mexican nationals who officially immigrated to the United States was only around 350. The demographic impact of such small numbers on the Mexican-American population was very minor. However, this changed dramatically after 1900, especially in the two decades between 1910 and 1930. While much of this immigration may have been provoked by the horror of the Mexican Revolution, there were also significant incentives for American business interests to invite Mexican laborers to fill the labor vacuum.

When the Dominguez family crossed the border at the end of 1909, they were part of the first wave of Mexican immigration to America. By first wave, I mean that my family came to the United States shortly before the Mexican Revolution started. This civil war that commenced in 1910 unleashed a series of bloody campaigns that touched every part of the Republic and destroyed at least a million lives.

MEXICAN IMMIGRATION, 1848-1930

The migration of Mexican nationals to the United States prior to 1910 primarily stemmed from both "push" and "pull" factors. The 1882 Chinese Exclusion Act and the 1907 Gentlemen's Agreement with Japan had led to the virtual exclusion of Chinese and Japanese laborers from the railroad, construction, and agricultural industries.

According to the historian Juan R. Garcia, the author of *Mexicans in the Midwest, 1900-1932*, "a curtailment of immigration from Asia and the Europeans' preference for year-round employment and higher wages had led to a severe labor shortage." To fill the void left in their work forces, the railroad companies began an aggressive campaign to enlist Mexican labor for their work forces.[3]

---

[3] Juan R. Garcia, *Mexicans in the Midwest, 1900 – 1932* (Tucson: The University of Arizona Press, 1996), p. 6; Judith Fincher Laird, *Argentine, Kansas: The Evolution of a Mexican-American Community, 1905-1940* (University of Kansas, Ph.D., 1975), pp. 26-27.

By 1900, the railway trackage of Mexico had increased to over 12,000 miles, with several major lines reaching the northern border zone. Juan R. Garcia observed that "an unexpected outcome of this construction was that it drew thousands of Mexican workers steadily northward as the lines advanced toward the border." Continuing with this line of thought, Mr. Garcia wrote, "For many the railroad represented employment and an avenue of escape. By 1900 Mexico's principal railroads were completed and connected to the major American railways lines along the border."[4]

In his work *Rebirth: Mexican Los Angeles from the Great Migration to the Great Depression*, the historian Douglas Monroy explains that "the farther north one traveled the higher the wages." As an example, Professor Monroy pointed out that in pre-Revolutionary Jalisco, "agricultural workers received 12 cents per day, with an allotment of maize. Fifteen cents was the maximum

---

[4] Juan R. Garcia, *op. cit.*, p. 6.

pay per day." However, in stark contrast, the section hands working along the Mexican National Railway earned fifty cents per day. At the same time, the Mexican Central Railroad was paying between seventy-five and eighty cents a day in the state of Chihuahua. Railroad laborers working near the border city of Ciudad Juárez even received a dollar a day. And, as Professor Monroy concludes, "In the north of Mexico, wages were roughly double what they were in the interior."[5]

However, as Mexican laborers took the higher paying jobs in the Chihuahua, they quickly learned that railroad laborers in the U.S. could earn $1.00 to $1.25 a day. With this incentive, many laborers simply crossed the border to take advantage of the better wages. Mr. Larry Rutter, in his Master's Thesis at Kansas State University, pointed out that "wage differentials, especially among common labor, were so great between the two countries, that many

---

[5] Douglas Monroy, *Rebirth: Mexican Los Angeles from the Great Migration to the Great Depression* (Berkeley: University of California, 1999), p. 90.

persons could make more money by working three months in the United States than in a whole year in Mexico. Wage rates before the Revolution in 1910 were as low as twenty-five cents a day with little hope for advancement."[6]

Many Mexican laborers were qualified to take on railroad jobs in the United States because of their prior experience in Mexican railroad work. In addition, many employers actively sought Mexican labor because they perceived the Mexican laborers as docile, hard-working people who did not complain about low wages and poor working conditions.

"Their desirability as laborers," writes Mr. Garcia, "was augmented by the employers' belief that most returned to Mexico once the job had ended. Before long Mexicans were laying tracks

---

[6] Larry G. Rutter, *Mexican Americans in Kansas: A Survey and Social Mobility Study, 1900-1970* (Master's Thesis, Kansas State University, Manhattan, 1972), p. 11.

and constructing roadbeds for most of the major rail lines. Once this work had been completed, many remained in the United States as track maintenance crews."[7]

American immigration records indicate that between 1900 and 1904, only 2,259 Mexicans legally crossed the border to look for work. However, in the next five-year period from 1905 to 1909, this figure increased almost tenfold to 21,732 individual crossings. From 1910 to 1914, the number of entries increased to an unprecedented 82,588, in large part due to the depredations of the Mexican Revolution (which had started in 1910).[8]

The number Mexicans legally crossing the border between 1915 and 1919 reached 91,075, at a time when Mexican labor became even more important because American soldiers marching off to World War I battlefields in Europe had created a labor shortage.

---

[7] Juan R. Garcia, *op. cit.*, p. 6.

[8] Judith Fincher Laird, *op. cit.*, p. 66.

MEXICAN IMMIGRATION, 1848-1930

From July 1910 to July 1920, an estimated 890,371 legal Mexican immigrants came to the United States. Between 1920 and 1924, 249,248 Mexicans entered the country, with 1924 as the peak year (when 89,336 immigrants entered the country).[9]

The increasing trend of Mexican immigration continued for the rest of the 1920s with 238,527 entries recorded between 1925 and 1929. During this period, Mexican immigrants would comprise 15.68% of all immigrants to the U.S.[10] During the 1920s, six major railroads employed between 32,000 and 42,000 Mexican track workers, depending on the season. These laborers comprised 75% of the total track force.[11]

---

[9] *Ibid.*; U.S. Bureau of Census, *The Statistical History of the United States from Colonial Times to the Present* (Stamford, Conn.: Fairfield Publishers, Inc., 1947), pp. 58-59.

[10] Judith Fincher Laird, *op. cit.*, p. 66.

[11] Mark Reisler, *op. cit.*, p. 96.

MEXICAN IMMIGRATION, 1848-1930

In 1910, the U.S. Census Bureau enumerated 221,915 Mexican-born nationals, but estimated the total "Mexican race" population at 367,510, including citizens of Mexican parents born in the United States. As the economies of the southwestern United States boomed, Mexicans flocked into the region, nearly half of them to Texas and more than one-fourth to California. When the revolution erupted in Mexico on November 25, 1910, almost 2.5 percent of native-born Mexicans were already living with the borders of the United States.

The late author, Carey McWilliams, in his work *North from Mexico*, cited the period of 1900-1912 as the peak of the railroads' recruitment of Mexicans in the United States.   Nine western railroads listed 5,972 workers – or 17.1 percent of the workforce – as Mexicans in 1909. Twenty years later, these railroads employed 22,824 Mexicans, or 59.5 percent of their common labor force.[12]

---

[12] Paul S. Taylor, "Some Aspects of Mexican Immigration," *Journal of Political Economy* 38 (October 1930), p. 611.

MEXICAN IMMIGRATION, 1848-1930

In the 1920s, the anthropologist, Manuel Gamio, conducted studies to determine where most of the Mexican immigrants were coming from. Using oral interviews and statistical date, Dr. Gamio discovered that the largest group of immigrants to America came from the Central Plateau region of Mexico, primarily the states of Jalisco, Michoacán, Guanajuato, Zacatecas and Aguascalientes, where the agricultural situation was the least favorable to the average Mexican peon.[13]

By 1910, Mexican immigration to the United States had become an important component of the economy of several American states. My family was recruited by the Santa Fe Railroad and made its way to the Texas Panhandle, in the hopes of making a decent living and putting food on the table.

---

[13] Manual Gamio, *Mexican Immigration to the United States* (Chicago: University of Chicago Press, 1930), p. 34.

A STOP-OVER IN TEXAS

The Texas Panhandle

The details of my family's journey from El Paso to the Panhandle of Texas are not known. My Aunt Felicitas Dominguez Morales was the last living person who made the journey, but she died in 1988, so we have no living witnesses to tell us about this journey. My family's last home in Mexico was the city of Mapimí, located in the Laguna District of the state of Durango, some 64 kilometers (40 miles) northwest of Gómez Palacio. Felicitas was born in Mapimí in August 1909 and – four months later – her parents, Geronimo and Luisa – carried her across the border at El Paso.

We do not know how long the two Dominguez families stayed in El Paso, but we know that it was not a very long time. During this period, the railroad and agricultural industries of the Panhandle Region of Northern Texas were rapidly expanding. The resulting economic boom required the importation of laborers into the region. The Santa Fe Railroad – which already had routes connecting El Paso to Kansas City – had begun actively recruiting

Mexican laborers to maintain their railways through the Panhandle.

Bordered by New Mexico on the west and Oklahoma on the north and east, the Texas Panhandle consists of approximately 26,000 square miles – roughly the size of West Virginia – and is actually larger than nine American states. In all, the Panhandle is composed of twenty-six counties and sixty-two incorporated towns and represents the northern extension of Texas' Great Plains region.[1] The Panhandle Region – from its earliest settlement – has been on a fast track as a major producer of cattle. This part of the state has also developed into a major producer of wheat and contains huge natural gas resources. The Panhandle would – for several years – become the home of the Dominguez family.

---

[1] Amarillo Convention and Visitors Council, 2001.

A STOP-OVER IN TEXAS

Amarillo

For more than a century, the City of Amarillo has been the cultural and economic center of the Texas Panhandle. Amarillo is located on the boundary of Potter and Randall Counties and is the county seat of Potter County. Today, the City is located at the crossroads of Interstate Highway 40 and Interstate Highway 27. Amarillo is approximately 580 kilometers (360 miles) northwest of Dallas-Fort Worth, 459 kilometers (285 miles) east of Albuquerque, New Mexico, and 427 kilometers (265 miles west) of Oklahoma City, Oklahoma.

Originally settled in 1887, Amarillo was incorporated as a city in 1892. The name Amarillo was taken from the Spanish language meaning "yellow," because of the color of the soil found in the channel of the Amarillo Creek. Thanks to the Panhandle's production of cattle, Amarillo remains one of the largest cattle-shipping markets in the country even today. It was the coming of the railroad to the Panhandle that made Amarillo into a major transportation and distribution center even in the Nineteenth Century.

In 1886, the Southern Kansas Railway Company, an affiliate of the AT&SF Railroad Company, began construction of a line from Kiowa, Kansas, across Indian Territory (Oklahoma) to the Texas border. The thirty miles of the Southern Kansas Railway from the Oklahoma-Texas border to the City of Canadian was put into service in September 1887.[2] A year later, the railroad arrived in Amarillo, making this town the most important marketing center for ranchers in the Panhandle area. By 1899, the Santa Fe Railroad had established a large division office in Amarillo and built an engine house, a machine shop and blacksmith shop. By 1900, Amarillo already had a population of 1,442, which increased dramatically to 9,957 persons in 1910.[3]

[2] "PANHANDLE AND SANTA FE RAILWAY." The Handbook of Texas Online.
<http://www.tsha.utexas.edu/handbook/online/articles/view/PP/eqp3.html>

[3] "AMARILLO, TX." The Handbook of Texas Online.
<http://www.tsha.utexas.edu/handbook/online/articles/view/AA/hda2.html>

A STOP-OVER IN TEXAS

Canadian, Texas

The Dominguez family has always claimed that our family lived in Amarillo, Texas before they came to Kansas City. But the 1910 Federal Census found the Dominguez clan in Canadian Texas, a 193 kilometers (120 miles) northeast of Amarillo. Canadian is the county seat of Hemphill County, Texas and is located eight to ten miles northwest of the center of the county. Hemphill County – like most of the Panhandle Region – was originally populated by Apache Indians, who were pushed out in the late Eighteenth Century by the Kiowas and Comanches.

With the arrival of the railroad in 1887, Canadian quickly developed a reputation as the "Rodeo Town" after the annual Cowboys' Reunion was first staged in the town in 1888.[4] In 1907,

---

[4] For information relating to Canadian, Texas the authors recommend the following works: F. Stanley [Stanley F. L. Crocchiola], *The Canadian, Texas, Story* (Nazareth, Texas, 1975) and F. Stanley [Stanley F. L. Crocchiola], *Rodeo Town (Canadian, Texas)* (Denver: World, 1953).

A STOP-OVER IN TEXAS

Canadian became a railroad division point. This activity was responsible for a large influx of laborers from other areas.[5]

A New Home in America

When the census taker arrived at the doorstep of my great-grandfather, Aniceto Dominguez, on May 2, 1910, the Dominguez household in Enumeration District 138 of the Canadian Township of the State of Texas contained seven family members. Aniceto Dominguez was incorrectly listed in the Federal Census as "Anesto Domingus" and was classified as a 48-year-old Mexican-born railway worker. He stated that he had arrived in the U.S. in 1909 and had been married to his wife for seven years.

Aniceto's wife, Dorotea "Domingus" gave her age was 21. The three children of Aniceto and Dorotea were listed as follows: Carlota (5 years old), Martina (4 years old) and Milkios (1 year

---

[5] CANADIAN, TX." The Handbook of Texas Online.
<http://www.tsha.utexas.edu/handbook/online/articles/view/CC/hgc2.html>
[Accessed Sun Jun 15 23:46:31 US/Central 2003].

old). It is important to note that the language barrier between an Anglo census taker and a Spanish-speaking family frequently led to misspellings of names or misunderstandings about names.

Geronimo Dominguez was tallied in Aniceto's household as a 24-year-old railway laborer. Geronimo's wife Luisa was listed as Aniceto's 21-year-old daughter-in-law. For some reason, the census states that Luisa had given birth to two children but none of her children were living. I am not sure where Pablo and Felicitas Dominguez were at the time of this census, but I do know that they were alive, possibly living with other relatives. Once again, this may have been a misunderstanding between the English-speaking census taker and the Spanish-speaking family he interviewed.

Within a year or two, the Dominguez family resettled in Amarillo. Geronimo continued working for the Santa Fe Railroad in the "run house" where train engines were repaired. After a couple of years, however, Geronimo was hurt in an accident. Because of this injury, Geronimo had to give up railroad work, forcing the family to sell tamales for a living. The making of the tamales was a family effort, and a neighborhood friend, Mariana, helped them in their new business.[6]

During their stay in Amarillo, Geronimo and Luisa added more children to their family. On January 1, 1912, Jesus Maria Dominguez (my Uncle Jesse) was born. He was baptized on March 8, 1912 at the Sacred Heart Church in Amarillo, with Guadalupe Hidalgo and Porfiria Hidalgo as his godparents.

Two years later, Luisa gave birth to her fourth child (and second daughter), Juliana, who was born on January 29, 1914 in Amarillo. The next child born after Juliana was Uncle Raul, who was followed on January 15, 1918 by my mother, Pabla Dominguez.

---

[6] Louie Gonzales, *The Dominguez – Chavez Family History* (Kansas City, 2000), p. 5.

A STOP-OVER IN TEXAS

Although my mother had originally been given the name Pabla, she has been called Bessie for much of her life.

Early in the Twentieth Century, the reputation of Amarillo, Texas as an important commercial center continued to grow. And, as a result, much of the economy of the Panhandle area revolved around this city. However, when the United States became involved in World War I in April 1917, Amarillo also became a production center for the war effort. My family and most Americans watched the progress of the warfare as French, British and American forces battled the German troops in the trenches northeast of Paris.

Soon, the terror of chemical warfare became widely publicized in the press. Rumors were spread with great frequency as Americans began to realize that the dangerous chemicals being used in the European front were being produced at locations within the U.S. From the earliest years of the Twentieth Century, Texas – with its rich resources of natural gas – became the chosen location for several chemical industries. Amarillo – with its strategic location along railroad routes – became an important producer of chemicals.[7]

It was during this period that my family sensed a serious problem in Amarillo. According to my Uncle Jessie, sometime in 1917, almost everyone in the entire town of Amarillo became sick, supposedly from mustard gas. My family, to this day, believes that experiment in biological warfare were taking place in the area around Amarillo and that these dangerous texts were responsible for the wide-spread illness that affected everyone in the area.

Considering that gas warfare was legal in these days, this theory seems to be a valid one. During this time, the youngest child of the family, Raul, became very ill and died when the doctors prescribed

[7] M. A. M. Anari and Jared E. Hazelton, *The Chemical Industry of Texas* (College Station: Center for Business and Economic Analysis, Texas A&M University, 1992).

the wrong medicine for him. The suspicious events taking place during this time prompted Aniceto and Geronimo to move their families to Kansas City.

Around the second half of 1917, an Amarillo photographer stopped by the Dominguez household and offered to take a photograph of the children for a small fee. Pablo, Felicitas, Jessie and little Juliana – who was only three years old – were assembled by their mother for the photograph. The resulting picture – provided to us by Louie Gonzales – shows four children gazing into the camera lens. It was not long after this that my mother Pabla was born. And very soon after her birth, the entire Dominguez family moved on to Kansas City, where they expected to find gainful employment in the meatpacking business.

The Dominguez Children (Amarillo, Texas, 1917)

From left to right, Jessie, Julia, Felicitas, Pablo

RIDING THE RAILS TO KANSAS

Kansas[1]

Pabla Dominguez was the fifth child born in the family of Geronimo and Luisa Lujan Dominguez in January 1918. World War I was being waged overseas and American troops were marching off in ever increasing numbers to fight the Axis Powers (Germany, Austria-Hungary, Bulgaria and the Ottoman Empire). With so many American men marching off to war, the need for migrant Mexican labor became more pronounced than ever. The war had brought immigration from Europe almost to a standstill, and American laws continued to discourage the influx of most Asian laborers.

With the production of wartime materials at a peak, businesses in many parts of the United States turned to the Mexican migrant to fill their needs. My family soon found out about new

---

[1] The authors thank Ms. Cynthia Mines for permission to use the title of her book *Riding the Rails to Kansas: The Mexican Immigrants* as the title to this chapter: Cynthia Mines, *Riding the Rails to Kansas: The Mexican Immigrants* (Kansas, 1980).

opportunities for employment in Kansas City. Aniceto Dominguez, my great-grandfather, was now approaching the age of sixty and could not maintain the rigorous workload of a railroad laborer. My grandfather Geronimo – because of his previous work injury and his chronic cough – also needed to find a different source of income.

So early in 1918, Aniceto moved his family to the West Bottoms Barrio in Ward I of Kansas City to start working for the Ice Plant in the Argentine district of Kansas City. Soon after Geronimo followed with his wife and family. When the Dominguez family made their way to "The Bread Basket of America" (as Kansas was called in those days), they were part of a growing migration to the Heartland of America.

The state of Kansas has a rectangular shape (except for its northeastern corner that borders the Missouri River). Kansas became the thirty-fourth American state in 1861 and – as the western boundaries of the nation shifted to the Pacific coast – moved to a central position within the United States. In spite of its all American image, Kansas – like many other American states – is derived from a Native American word. The word *Kansas* was donated to the English language by the Kansas, or Kaw, Indians, who once roamed the prairies of this region. In their language, *Kansa* meant "People of the South Wind."

Kansas City

Kansas City, Kansas is an industrial city located in the northeast corner of the state of Kansas along the Kansas-Missouri border. With twelve railroads entering its environment from all directions, Kansas City continues to boast a large manufacturing sector. It was the railroad that first brought so much attention to Kansas City. The 1880s were a decade of rapid construction of rails throughout the state, with the Atchison, Topeka and Santa Fe Railroad connecting Kansas City directly to El Paso way back in 1884.

RIDING THE RAILS TO KANSAS

According to the author and editor, Cynthia Mines, "The railroad brought to Kansas a new age in transportation" and an "exposure to a different culture and people, an ethnic experience not welcomed by everyone in the small Kansas towns early in the century."[2] The 1900 Federal Census had tallied a mere seventy-one 71 Mexican-born individuals as residents of the state of Kansas.

The Santa Fe Railroad, the Chicago, Rock Island and Pacific Railroad, and the Brownsville-Kansas City Railway line – constructed in 1904 – became the principal conduits for the migration of Mexican labor early in the century. As early as 1903, the Santa Fe Railroad, headquartered in Topeka, had begun hiring Mexicans, although it was not until 1907 that the company actively recruited Mexicans from Texas.[3]

---

[2] *Ibid.*, Preface.

[3] Larry Rutter, *Mexican Americans in Kansas*, Master's Thesis (Kansas State University, 1972), p. 46.

RIDING THE RAILS TO KANSAS

Many Kansas cities recorded their first significant influx of Mexicans between 1905 and 1910. Initially most Mexican laborers were hired as section crews, who worked from May to October and then returned to Mexico. By 1910, fifty-five percent of all track laborers in Kansas City were Mexicans, a figure that increased to 85% in 1915 and to more than 91% in 1927.[4]

Eventually, the Santa Fe Railroad became the largest employer of Mexican labor in Kansas. According to figures released by a national railroad official to the U.S. Senate Committee on Immigration, the Santa Fe and the Southern Pacific railroads employed almost 20,000 Mexican track laborers in 1928.[5]

---

[4] Juan R. Garcia, *op. cit.*, pp. 6-7, 117; Judith Fincher Laird, *Argentine, Kansas: The Evolution of a Mexican-American Community, 1905-1940* (Doctorate Dissertation, University of Kansas, 1975), p. 117; John Martínez, *Mexican Emigration to the U.S.* (San Francisco: R and E Research Associates, 1971), p. 4.

[5] Larry Rutter, *op. cit.*, p. 74.

RIDING THE RAILS TO KANSAS

A Burgeoning Mexican Community in the Heartland

It is believed that the first Mexican settlement in Kansas City was constructed in 1905, when a "barrio" cropped up in the flood-prone Argentine District, which was made up mostly of abandoned boxcars – provided by the Santa Fe Railroad – and a scattering of small boarding houses. Of the first 300 Mexicans living in Argentine, two hundred worked for the railroad, while 12% percent were women and another 12% were children.[6]

According to the 1910 census, most of the 8,429 foreign-born Mexicans living in Kansas were employed by the railroad. In this year, only Texas, California, Arizona, and New Mexico had more Mexican immigrants than Kansas. Dr. Valerie Marie Mendoza, in her PhD dissertation, *The Creation of a Mexican Immigrant Community in Kansas City, 1890-1930*, writes that Mexican

---

[6] Valerie M. Mendoza, "They Came to Kansas: Searching for a Better Life," 25 Kansas Quarterly 97-106 (1994), Notes 74 and 75; Lin Fredericksen, "Fiesta, Kansas Style, A Moment in Time" Kansas State Historical Society (September 2001) (available at http://www.kshs.org/features/feat901.htm).

laborers "came in such large numbers that the 1920 federal census listed Kansas as containing the fifth largest Mexican population of any state in the U.S."[7]

As political instability continued to grip Mexico for the entire decade from 1910 to 1920, Mexican immigrants were becoming less and less inclined to return home. This, coupled with the labor shortage created by World War I and the restrictions on European immigration that were in effect, swelled the number of Mexicans in Kansas to 13,770 in 1920 and 19,042 by 1930. In some areas, the railroad officials actually started to encourage the Mexican men to send for their families so that they would settle permanently and form a more stable work labor force. As a result, real communities started to take shape. In some areas, Mexicans

---

[7] Valerie Marie Mendoza, *The Creation of a Mexican Immigrant Community in Kansas City, 1890-1930* (PhD Dissertation, University of California at Berkeley, 1997), pp. viii – ix.

119

established their own parishes and organized fiestas and other celebrations centering around their churches and cultural events.[8]

During the second decade of the Twentieth Century, a new incentive for Mexican migration to Mexico emerged. For more than a century, Kansas City has had one of the largest meat packing industries in the country. Because of the close proximity of the large cattle raising regions and hog markets and because of Kansas City's rapid growth as a Midwest railroad center, the meat packing industry became one of the most important economic forces in the area.[9]

Probably the most famous packing plant in Kansas City was the Armour Brothers Packing House, organized by members of the Armour family in the 1880s. The company name was later changed to Armour Packing Company and in 1910 to Armour and

---

[8] Larry Rutter, *op. cit.,* pp. 45, 74; Cynthia Mines, *op. cit.,* p. 2.

[9] The Kansas City *Kansan,* November 24, 1985: p 2A.

Company. When my grandfather Geronimo arrived in Kansas
City, Armour became his first employer. By 1924, the Kansas
City *Kansan* was reporting that "Kansas City has become the
second meat packing center in the world. It is the only city in
which all the large packing companies have established plants."[10]

The Kansas packing plants first started to hire Mexican labor
around 1914. Then, with the increased product demand and labor
shortage caused by World War I, the packing plants started to
recruit larger numbers of migrants as employees. Unfortunately,
most of the jobs offered to Mexican immigrants were unskilled
and low-paying positions. Dr. Mendoza writes that these jobs
"included everything from salter to beef skinner to sheep killer to
working in the freezer. Those who worked as laborers in the
killing department most likely cleaned blood from the floor."[11]

---

[10] *Ibid.,* Oct. 15, 1924.

[11] Valerie Marie Mendoza, *The Creation of a Mexican Immigrant Community in Kansas City, 1890-1930,* pp. 78-79.

However, Dr. Mendoza observes that "as with the railroad industry, work in the packing houses was highly labor intensive and seasonal. Mexicans were not guaranteed year-round work with the slack season occurring during the summer months. Packing companies, therefore, hired most Mexican laborers on a short-term basis."[12]

By 1915, Dr. Mendoza writes, "two distinct" Mexican-American settlements had taken shape in Kansas City. The first settlement was Argentine, which lay close to the Santa Fe railroad tracks. The development of the Argentine area was discussed in detail in Judith Fincher Laird's dissertation, *Argentine, Kansas: The Evolution of a Mexican-American Community, 1905-1940.* This report, submitted in 1975 to the Department of History at the University of Kansas, examined and analyzed the development of the Mexican-American barrio in Argentine in the pre-1940 period. Mr. Laird's work Ms. Laird's work was also produced in 1977 by

---

[12] *Ibid.*, p. 79.

University Microfilms International, Ann Arbor, Michigan, by microfilm-xerography.

A second major Mexican settlement developed in the "West Bottoms Barrio" – the old warehouse and stockyard area just below the Downtown Kansas City bluffs. This settlement soon began to attract migrant populations. At the turn of the century, some 200 acres of slaughterhouses and packinghouses dotted the West Bottoms area.

In her work, Dr. Mendoza refers to the West Bottoms as "the working man's neighborhood population by the city's few foreign-born residents (mostly of East European origin) and Anglo laborers, all of whom worked at the railroad tracks, packing houses, and other industries in the neighborhood. The West Bottoms was an extremely transient section of town, whose temporary residents, including Mexicans, were accommodated by boarding houses and residence hotels."[13]

As we mentioned above, when my great-grandfather Aniceto Dominguez first arrived in Kansas around 1918, he found a place for his family to stay in the West Bottoms Barrio and started to work for the Ice Plant in Argentine. My grandfather Geronimo followed soon after and he too went to work in the meat packing industry of Kansas City. As it turns out, nearly all of their fellow countrymen found similar employment. By 1921, the meat packing industry in Kansas City employed between 200 and 300 Mexicans, many of whom lived in West Bottoms.[14]

---

[13] *Ibid.*, pp. 50-51; 1920 Kansas City Directory and Business Catalog (Kansas City: Gale City Directory Company, 1920); Lyle W. Dorsett, *The Pendergast Machine* (Lincoln: University of Nebraska Press, 1968).

[14] Judith Fincher Laird, *op. cit.*, p. 39.

RIDING THE RAILS TO KANSAS

In addition to the professional challenges they faced, the Mexican immigrant had to cope with a very personal challenge. Dr. Mendoza observed that the Mexican migrants to Kansas had a very different experience than their brethren in Texas. What they experienced in Kansas City was basically a form of culture shock, as Dr. Mendoza detailed in her dissertation:[15]

> Unlike migrants to the border region, those who journeyed inland did not have a host community to welcome them and help them to adjust to this foreign country.... Settling in the heart of the country was much more difficult for Mexican migrants. Compared to southwestern cities... Kansas City was extremely homogeneous, with a foreign born population no greater than nine percent, and that nine percent was made up of European ethnic groups...
>
> Most of the population, therefore consisted of U.S. citizens – Kansas City was not an immigrant town, and these Kansas Citians had never come into contact with Mexicans... Mexicans, for their part, had to learn to navigate this new and strange environment on their own. They learned about American and Kansas City prejudices by trial and error. They looked different, they talked funny, they dressed oddly, and they ate unrecognizable foods. Because

---

[15] Valerie Marie Mendoza, *The Creation of a Mexican Immigrant Community in Kansas City, 1890-1930*, pp. viii – ix.

> of the color of their skin and their foreign status, Mexicans found that certain establishments (bars, restaurants, rooming houses, stores, etc.) did not welcome them. Mexicans, therefore, quickly discovered where they were and were not allowed.

Continuing with this line of thought, Dr. Mendoza explained that "Mexican migrants faced an alien environmental landscape... Instead of fresh air, the mercado, and the plaza, Mexicans were greeted by the noise of train whistles, the sight of smoke and soot, and the stench of cattle and hogs. No longer did they cross paths with people they knew since childhood, the familiar faces of neighbors, compadres, relatives, wives, family as they journeyed from home to field or to the town square."[16]

The Dominguez Family in Kansas

Our first record of Geronimo Dominguez as a resident of Kansas City comes from his Draft Registration Card. When he registered for the draft on September 12, 1918, Geronimo gave 78 North

---

[16] *Ibid.*, p. 51.

First Street, Kansas City, Kansas as his permanent home address. He described himself as a laborer for Armour Packing Company and said that "Louisa Dominguez' was his "nearest relative." The registration also describes Geronimo as having a slender build, black eyes, and black hair. The registrar signing the card, Lillie Babbith, also observed that my grandfather was tall.

Some time later, we have been told, Geronimo went to work for another packing house owned by Swift and Company. Starting a few years later, Geronimo would also take part in seasonal work by laboring in the beet fields of Mitchell, Nebraska with other Mexican nationals. As the children grew older, the entire family would take trip and all would be put to work in the fields.

In the 1920 Federal Census, Aniceto Dominguez was listed as the 64-year-old head of household at 61 North First Street in Precinct 2, Enumeration District 153, Kansas City, Wyandotte County, Kansas. By this time, Aniceto's wife, Dorotea, had died, apparently after the birth of their son, Manuel Dominguez, on January 25, 1917. Thus, the two-time widower Aniceto Dominguez now headed a household of five. His four children were tallied as follows: Carlota (daughter, 16 years old, born in Mexico); Melgara (son, 11 years old, born in Mexico); Rosie (daughter, 8 years old, born in Texas); and Ned (son, 6 years old, born in Kansas). Aniceto told the census-taker that he was employed as a laborer in a packinghouse.

Aniceto's son, 38-year-old Geronimo Dominguez, lived close by at 78 North First Street and headed a household of seven family members and two boarders. By this time, Luisa was 32 years old. The children listed in the household were Paul (son, 14 years old), Feliz (daughter, 9 years old), Jesus (son, 7 years old), Pablamante (daughter, 5 years old), and Albera (son, 2 years and one month in age). We believe that the five-year-old Pablamante must have been Aunt Juliana, since she was older than my mother, Pabla. And, it is likely that my mother Pabla is probably the two-year-old son, Albera (another miscalculation lost in the translation). Frequently, Anglo census-takers misunderstood the people they interviewed when they spoke a foreign tongue. The first two children gave Mexico as their place of birth, while the last three were listed as natives of Texas.

According to estimates provided by Judith Fincher Laird, 17.86 percent of the Mexican laborers in Kansas City during the 1920s gave Zacatecas as their state of origin.[17] In contrast, Manuel Gamio, writing in *Mexican Immigration to the United States*, stated that in 1926 immigrants from Zacatecas made up only 4.8% of the total Mexican immigrant population in the United States.[18] Ms. Laird writes that the largest number of immigrants to Kansas were from Guanajuato (31.25%) and Michoacán (25.89%). After Zacatecas, the other states contributing immigrants to Kansas were

---

[17] Judith Fincher Laird, *op. cit.*, p. 88.

[18] Manual Gamio, *Mexican Immigration to the United States: A Study of Human Migration and Adjustment* (Chicago: The University of Chicago Press, 1930), p. 13.

Jalisco (9.82%), Durango (3.57%), Aguascalientes (2.68%), and
Coahuila (2.68%).[19]

On the following page we have reproduced a map from *The
Routledge Historical Atlas of the American Railroads*, to illustrate
the many Santa Fe rail lines that run through Texas, Oklahoma,
Kansas, and other adjacent states.[20]   In effect, the Santa Fe
Railroad and other railways paved the way for my ancestors and
many other Mexican-American families to move through the
United States in search of suitable jobs.

---

[19] Judith Fincher Laird, *op. cit.*, p. 88.

[20] Copyright © 1999 from John F. Stover, *The Routledge Historical Atlas of the
American Railroads: Routledge Atlases of American History* (New York:
Routledge, 1999), p. 91. Reproduced by permission of Routledge/ Taylor &
Francis Books, Inc.

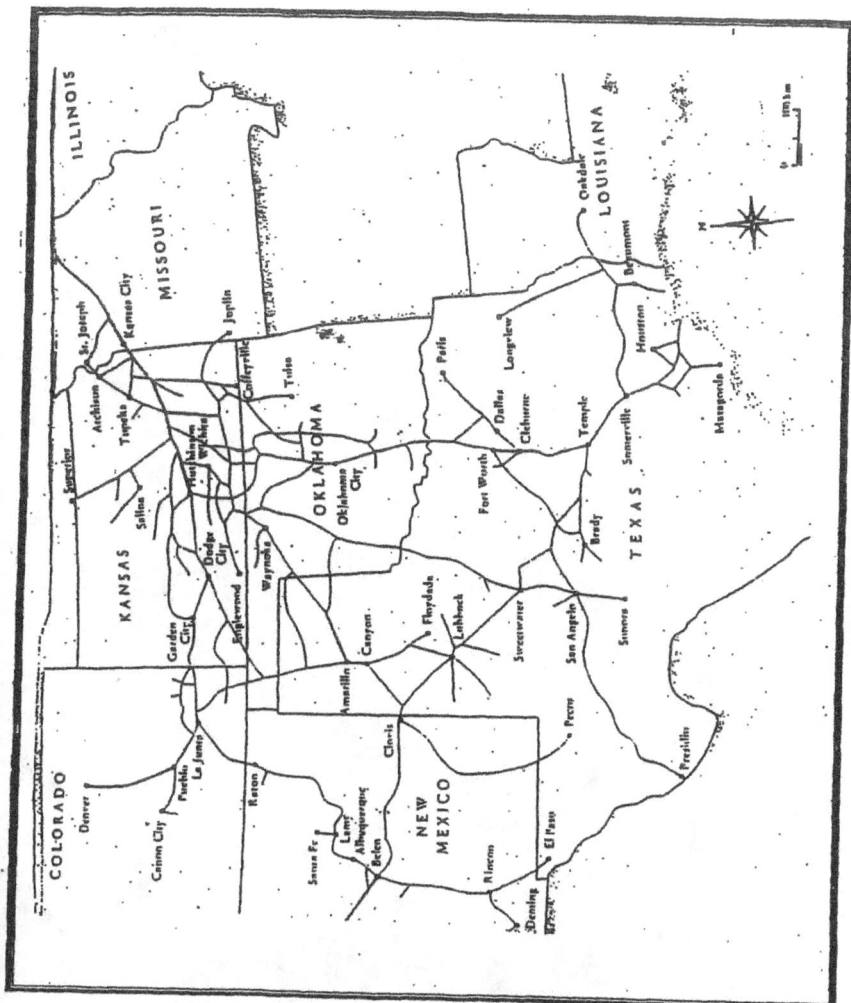

*The Santa Fe Railways (Reproduced by permission of Routledge/
Taylor & Francis Books, Inc.)*

A DIFFICULT LIFE

A New Decade

During the 1920s, my grandmother Luisa Lujan de Dominguez gave birth to several more children, starting with the delivery of a little infant girl, Ephifania (Effie) Dominguez, born on April 7, 1920 as the first Dominguez child born in Kansas. Two years later, on May 19, 1922, Uncle Erminio would follow Aunt Effie into the family lineup.

After another two years, my next uncle, Marshall Dominguez, born on July 3, 1924, would be welcomed into the family circle. But, with each pregnancy, Luisa grew progressively weaker and more fragile. Luisa's last child, Louis Dominguez, would be born on July 20, 1926.

By this time, Luisa's general poor health and poor nutrition had led to serious complications. Although little Louie survived the birthing process, his mother experienced serious postpartum hemorrhage following childbirth. The doctor who cared for my grandmother at the time wrote that Luisa's "general poor health" was a contributory cause of death when he filled out the death certificate.[1]

My grandmother died at the age of 39 years, leaving her grieving and ailing husband Geronimo with nine children who ranged in age from 21 years (Pablo) to one day (Louis). The somber mood of the wake the next day has been captured on film. In the photograph on the following page, my grandfather Geronimo stands on the left. His half-sister Carlota (Aniceto's daughter) stands beside Geronimo. Next to Carlota stood Aunt Felicitas, holding the newborn infant, Louie. Aunt Julia stands at the right side of the photograph, flanked by a small portion of Uncle Erminio.[2]

---

[1] Certificate of Death, Wyandotte County, Kansas, Registered No. 21442.

[2] We thank Louie Gonzales and the Jesse Dominguez family for permission to reproduce this family photograph; Louie Gonzales, *The Dominguez-Chavez Family History*, p. 26.

Geronimo Dominguez at the Funeral of Luisa, 1926

A DIFFICULT LIFE

Once Luisa had been buried in Maple Hill Cemetery, Geronimo returned home with his children. With the death of Luisa, my mother has said that, in these days, their lives became very difficult. It quickly became evident that Geronimo's employment could not entirely feed all the mouths at his kitchen table.

Because Geronimo was partially disabled, he would need to put his older children into the work force. Because Paul and Jessie and the girls were required to attend school, Geronimo could make not make them work all the year around yet. For the answer to his prayers, Geronimo looked to the beet fields of Nebraska.

Los Betabeleros

Back, in 1897 the U.S. Congress had imposed a large tariff on the importation of foreign sugar, thus encouraging the development of the U.S. sugar beet industry. As a result, by 1906, the amount of sugar beet acreage being farmed in the United States more than tripled from the 135,000 acres that had been planted in 1900. By

A DIFFICULT LIFE

1920 that acreage had increased to 872,000, with the Great Plains region (which includes the North Platte Valley in Wyoming and western Nebraska) producing 64 percent of the total crop grown in the U.S. From 1923 to 1932 Nebraska ranked second in the U.S., behind Colorado, in annual sugar beet acreage (74,000 acres), and first in the nation in yield per acre (12.7 tons).[3]

In 1905 there were only 250 acres of sugar beets in the entire North Platte Valley. In 1906 the Great Western Sugar Company started raising beets in that part of the state, and in just two years the increase in acreage warranted the building of a factory. At this time, Great Western's Ames, Nebraska factory was moved to

---

[3] Esther S. Anderson, *The Sugar Beet Industry of Nebraska* (Lincoln: Bulletin 9, Conservation Department of the Conservation and Survey Division, University of Nebraska, April, 1935), pp. 25-27.

Scottsbluff, Nebraska and enlarged. After that, Scotts Bluff County became the top sugar beet- producing county in Nebraska.[4]

During the last century, the city of Scottsbluff, Nebraska – located in Scotts Bluff County along the North Platte River in western Nebraska – was an important trading center for the North Ridge Platte River Irrigation Project. Scottsbluff lies only twenty miles from the border of Wyoming and represents the largest city in the so-called Western Nebraska Panhandle Region. As early as 1914, some Mexican laborers started to arrive in the Scottsbluff area and went to work in the sugar beet fields. As increasing numbers of migrants entered the area, the population of Scottsbluff increased to between five and six thousand inhabitants.

---

[4] *Ibid.*, pp. 21-22, 25; Dr. Ralph F. Grajeda, "Mexicans in Nebraska," (Lincoln, Nebraska: Nebraska State Historical Society, 1998) [Accessed online at <http://www.nebraskahistory.org/lib-arch/whadoin/mexampub/mexicans.htm>. Updated Oct 5, 1998.]

A DIFFICULT LIFE

Many of the *betabeleros* (sugar beet workers) came originally to the North Platte Valley as railroad hands, then, for a variety of reasons, changed jobs as more and more fieldwork became available. Few of these workers came to Nebraska directly from Mexico. The majority came from Kansas, others from Texas, Wyoming, Oklahoma, New Mexico, and Arizona. Kansas – with its burgeoning Mexican wartime community – became an important conduit for the moving of Mexican laborers to Nebraska.

After 1916, many of the *betabeleros* were aggressively recruited for labor in the beet fields by the Great Western Sugar Company. In 1915 the Great Western Sugar Company recruited and transported 500 workers into its Colorado, Wyoming, Montana, and Nebraska sugar beet territory. By 1920 this figure had increased to more than 13,000. In 1926 the Great Western Sugar Company provided transportation for 14,500 persons, employed fifty-five labor agents, and sent out advertising materials consisting of thousands of booklets, cardboard posters, and calendars-all in the Spanish language. Advertisements were run in fifteen newspapers located in various states.[5]

In Scottsbluff, a community developed near the Great Western Sugar refinery on land formerly owned by the factory and later sold to individual families. To this day, that area remains the Mexican American barrio in that city, bordered on the north by East Overland Drive, and on the south by South Beltline Road between Fifth and Fifteenth Avenues.[6]

Labor bosses in Nebraska started to recruit Mexican laborers from the Kansas City area to get some badly needed seasonal work done. When Geronimo and Aniceto learned that the beet growers

---

[5] Paul S. Taylor, *Mexican Labor in the United States*, Vol. I (New York: Arno Press and The New York Times, 1970), pp. 103, 105.

[6] Dr. Ralph F. Grajeda, "Mexicans in Nebraska," "Lincoln, Nebraska: Nebraska State Historical Society, 1998) [Accessed online at <http://www.nebraskahistory.org/lib-arch/whadoin/mexampub/mexicans.htm>. Updated Oct 5, 1998.]

A DIFFICULT LIFE

in Nebraska and Colorado would employ women and children in the fieldwork, they saw a great opportunity and an answer to their prayers for financial stability. Early in the century, a bounty of one dollar per ton harvest sugar beet had been offered to laborers. With a great need for workers of all ages to thin, hoe and harvest the sugar beets, all members of the family, including young children, were put to work during the thinning and weeding season.

In Scottsbluff, the migrant community developed near the Great Western Sugar refinery on land formerly owned by the factory. The town of Mitchell, which is located several miles west of Scottsbluff, became a second home for my family as many members of my mother's family worked here for a few months of the year. It was in Mitchell, Nebraska that some of my aunts and uncles met their future spouses. I know that my Uncle Jesse had met his wife Maria (Mary) Chavez in Mitchell in the early 1930s.[7]

---

[7] Louie Gonzales, *The Dominguez – Chavez Family History*, p. 42.

A DIFFICULT LIFE

Nineteen Thirty

For all these years, the Dominguez family kept one foot in the
door of Kansas City. When the census-taker arrived on April 22nd
at the doorstep of 68-year-old Aniceto Dominguez at Probst Road,
he provided the civil servant with the information he asked for.
Aniceto's name was spelled as "Anisito Dominguez" in Turner
Village of the Shawnce Township of Kansas City.[8]

Under the sections for "Home Data," Aniceto was described as
being the owner of his own home, which he valued at $1,000.
Nine family members lived in Aniceto's residence. Jeronimo
(Geronimo) Dominguez, listed as the son of a head of household,
gave his age as 46 years old. Geronimo's eldest son living at
home, Jesse was also listed as the "grandson" to the head of
household (Aniceto) and gave his age as 18. My 12-year-old

---

[8] The actual census schedules can be seen on National Archives Roll Number
T626-726, State of Nebraska, 1930, Page 12B, Enumeration District 73.

142

A DIFFICULT LIFE

mother, Bessie, was listed fourth as the "granddaughter" and followed by another granddaughter, Piero Dominguez, 10 years old (probably the incorrect spelling to Aunt Effie).

Eight-year-old Erminio (spelled "Ermono") was the next child listed in Aniceto's household, also tallied as a grandson to the head of the household. He was followed by still another grandson whose name was spelled Chale. This child was probably my Uncle Marshall, who was six years old at that time. Marshall was followed by Louis, the last grandson, whose age was given as 4 years and seven months of age. The last member of the household was 12-year-old Ned Dominguez, the son of Aniceto and his second wife, Dorotea, who was Geronimo's half-brother. Ned had been born in Amarillo about the same time that Uncle Jesse – his cousin – was born.

A DIFFICULT LIFE

According to this census, both Aniceto and Geronimo stated that they had immigrated to America in 1909 and that they were able to read and write, but could not speak the English language. While Aniceto was listed as having no occupation, Geronimo had given his occupation as "Section Hand" for the "Santa Fe RR" to which he had apparently found temporary employment in spite of his back problems. By this time, Geronimo's second-oldest son, Jesse, at the age 18, was also a "section hand" for the "Santa Fe Railroad."

Listed in one of the neighboring houses was the family of 30-year-old Frank Zamarripa, with his wife Nicolasa (26 years old) and his son, Isaiah (five years old). And listed in the next household was the Rangel family of Turner. Forty-five-year-old Antonino Rangel was the head of this family. Antonino had been born in La Calera Hacienda near Irapuato, Guanajuato and like so many other Guanajuato natives, he had made his way in 1915 to Kansas to start a new life. Living with him was his 35-year old wife,

A DIFFICULT LIFE

Concepcion Mosqueda, whose name was misspelled. Antonino also worked as a section hand for the Santa Fe Railroad. The Rangel family was one of the early Mexican-American families to make its home in the Turner District of Kansas City.

The Antonino and Concepcion Rangel family had four children at this time, who are listed as follows: Tony (son, 14 years old), Solomon (son, 8 years old), Esperse (daughter, 2 6/12 years old), and Doris (daughter, less than a year). The Rangel family, as neighbors, would befriend the Dominguez family.

Their young daughter, Esperanza (listed as Esperse) would play and spend time with the Dominguez children and has written a great deal about her memories of those bygone days. In addition to being a valuable source of information for our book, Esperanza has been an advocate for Hispanic causes for many years and has written a number of articles in the Kansas City *Star* and other newspapers about the struggle of Mexican Americans in Kansas City to earn respect from other ethnic groups.

Several other Mexican families were tallied up on that hill in Turner, Kansas, including 30-year-old Arvidio Aguilar (who immigrated in 1918), 28-year-old Domingo Galindo (who immigrated in 1918), and 31-year-old Raymond Loya (who immigrated in 1919). All of these gentlemen headed households in that neighborhood, and all of them worked as section hands for the railroads.

According to the 1930 census, my uncle Pablo Dominguez was living almost next door to Aniceto and Geronimo. Twenty-five-year-old Paul was listed as the head of household at the residence. His wife Manuela Dominguez was 26 years old and gave 1915 as her year of immigration to America. Their three small children were listed as: Isabella Dominguez (6 years old), Manuela Dominguez (4), and Olica Dominguez (1). It appears that Paul and Manuela had been married seven years earlier when he was 18 years old and when she was 19. Paul also worked as a section hand.

Uncle Paul was so much older than my mother and me that I remember very little about him. He was a coach cleaner and a painter for the Santa Fe Railroad Service for many years and became a member of the Brotherhood of Railroad Carmen. When he died on April 12, 1970 at the age of sixty-five, Uncle Paul was survived by his wife, Manuela, and four daughters: Ms. Dora Dominguez, Mrs. Isabel Quijas, and Mrs. Mary Garcia – all of Kansas – and Mrs. Alice Becerra of Detroit. He was also survived by two sons, Maynard and Robert Dominguez, who lived in Kansas City.

By this time my Aunt Julia Dominguez had also gone out on her own. While working in the beet fields of Nebraska, Julia had met her future husband, Eleno Salazar. Eleno – who as an adult became a naturalized citizen – was born in Leon, Guanajuato on August 18, 1908 as the eldest son of Salvador Salazar and Augustina Hernandez. When he was still an infant child, Salvador and Augustina brought Eleno across the border at El Paso on April 15, 1910. Because they had already been contracted for work, the Salazar family immediately went to the small town of Swink, Otero County, Colorado, which – even to this day – has a population of less than 700 people.

Located in southeastern Colorado along the Santa Fe Railroad, Swink profited when the sugar beet industry in Colorado took off early in the Twentieth Century. The Holly Beet Sugar Company was established in Swink and it was this business that employed the Salazar's and other Mexican migrant labor. The Salazar family lived in Swink, Colorado from April 1910 to December 1928, at which time, they moved on to the beet fields of Mitchell, Nebraska.

A DIFFICULT LIFE

It was in the beet fields of Mitchell that Eleno Salazar met my Juliana Dominguez. They were married on November 6, 1929 in Greeley, Colorado. Greeley was another stopover for Mexican migrants as the Greeley Sugar Company in that town employed many laborers. Juliana and Eleno made their home in Turner, Kansas from this point on. However, like the rest of the Dominguez extended family, the seasonal journey to work in Nebraska's beet fields continued through the early years of their marriage.

In the 1930 census, Juliana and Eleno were listed in the same household as Eleno's parents, Salvador and Augustina (Hernandez) Salazar. Thirty-eight-year-old Salvador Salazar headed this family in Ford Township, Scotts Bluff County, Nebraska.[9] Augustina was 42 years old and cared for the Eleno, Julia, and four other Salazar children. The first child of Eleno and

---

[9] The Salazar Family can be located on Roll T626_1292 in Nebraska Enumeration District Number 9, page 5A.

A DIFFICULT LIFE

Julian was Eleno Salazar, Jr., who was born on January 1, 1931 in Lyman, Nebraska. Their second child, Martha, was born in Mitchell, Nebraska on November 11, 1932. Eventually they would have four children, and Uncle Eleno eventually would work twenty-seven years as a clerk for the Santa Fe Railroad.

During this time, my mother's oldest sister, Felicitas Dominguez, met her future husband, Celestino Morales (who was the brother of my father, Daniel Morales). After they met, they were married and made a home for themselves in Argentine, Kansas, later moving on to Kansas City, Missouri, where they raised their family, while Celestino worked for the Nazarene Publishing House.

The Nineteen Thirties were the decade in which my family recognized itself as being a truly American family. There was no turning back now because most of the children had been born in America and had gone to school to learn English. Although many

A DIFFICULT LIFE

of my aunts and uncles were forced to leave school at an early age to labor in the beet fields, their identity as American citizens became well understood and a matter of pride. Although they spoke Spanish at home with their loved ones, the Dominguez family, in effect, lived and operated as an American family, working the railroads, attending church, and taking care of financial responsibilities. However, all this meant nothing to those people who saw my family as strangers in their native land. And the years to follow 1930 would be difficult years for my family.

SECOND-CLASS CITIZENS

Alien Inhabitants

By 1930, the Mexican and Mexican-American population of Kansas represented the seventh largest Mexican ancestral group in the entire U.S. They also comprised the second largest immigrant population in the state after Germans.[1] However, in spite of their increasing numbers, the author Cynthia Mines tells us that the "Mexican settlers were set apart linguistically, economically, religiously, and culturally from the mostly white, Protestant, middle class Kansans with which they were surrounded. They tended to stay within their colonies, some eventually building their own schools and churches, and ventured out only to buy necessities."[2]

Mexicans, according to Ms. Mines, "had a higher ethnic visibility, because of their darker skin complexion, and they were not as

---

[1] Robert Oppenheimer, "Acculturation or Assimilation: Mexican Immigrants in Kansas, 1900 to World War II," *The Western Historical Quarterly*, Vol. XVI, No. 1 (January 1985), p. 431.

[2] Cynthia Mines, *op. cit.*, p. 2.

easily assimilated into society as were the Germans, the largest immigrant group to Kansas."[3] Professor Robert Oppenheimer of the University of Kansas has described in some detail the segregation of and discrimination against Mexican Americans in Kansas:[4]

> Overt racial bias was common. Throughout Kansas, Mexicans remained segregated, and Anglos viewed Mexicans with suspicion even when they left the confines of the barrios for the day.... Until the 1950s, in virtually every Kansas town and city, Mexicans and Mexican-Americans remained segregated in movie theaters and were often restricted from some sections of city parks, churches, and other public facilities. Windows of some businesses contained signs stating "No Mexicans allowed," and Mexicans could not obtain haircuts in local barbershops.

Unfortunately, the segregation in Kansas included some churches. Although most Mexicans who arrived in Kansas were devout Catholics, they found some of the worst prejudice directed against them by fellow Catholics. As a rule, Mexican-American boys

---

[3] *Ibid.*, p. 6.

[4] Robert Oppenheimer, *op. cit.*, pp. 431-432.

were not permitted to serve as Catholic altar boys.[5] Ms. Mines lamented the fact that "Mexican Americans were not allowed to attend some masses and rather than be banished to the back of the church at services they did attend, many chose to worship in their own homes."[6]

In Search of God

Mission work by Baptists, Methodists and Presbyterians in the Mexican Barrios began in the early 1920s and had considerable success, especially with my family. Dr. Mendoza observed that eventually there were "no less than thirteen Protestant organizations engaged in 'Spanish-speaking work" in the state of Kansas.

Early on, "the Methodists established a mission in the Argentine barrio in order to improve conditions there during the 1921

---

[5] Interview with Esperanza Rangel Amayo, December 2002.

[6] Cynthia Mines, *op. cit.*, p. 91.

recession. It proved to be an important social service agency among Mexicans for three decades." Dr. Mendoza explains that "the Methodist Mission provided food, clothing, medical services, and monies and conducted educational, recreational, and religious activities. More importantly for women, it operated a daycare center and offered courses in sewing, cooking, and homemaking."[7]

Ms. Mines, in discussing the Protestant proselytizing efforts, writes "Some Mexican immigrants may have become Protestants because they had been helped in some material way by Protestant organizations – almost out of gratitude. Others, perhaps, were disillusioned as to the moral character of the Catholic priesthood, and they expected to find in the Protestant clergy pure, moral, unselfish men."[8]

---

[7] Valerie Marie Mendoza, *The Creation of a Mexican Immigrant Community in Kansas City, 1890-1930* (PhD Dissertation, University of California at Berkeley, 1997), pp. 131-132.

[8] Cynthia Mines, *op. cit.,* pp. 122-123.

SECOND-CLASS CITIZENS

Because Grandpa Geronimo had become very sickly from his years of working in silver mines, he had a terrible cough. When a locomotive door actually fell on him in Amarillo, his back injury had also further weakened him. But Geronimo was a man of great faith and sought the help of God and God's ministers. Uncle Jesse has explained to us that Geronimo met with a Methodist evangelist. The evangelist sold my grandfather a ticket that permitted him to go to a healing service.[9]

At this faith-healing service, Geronimo apparently felt much better and began to take a very enthusiastic interest in studying the bible. He healed enough from his earlier injuries that he was able to take on some carpentry work to help support his family. Because of his "reincarnation from bad health," Geronimo felt that this

---

[9] Louie Gonzales, *The Dominguez – Chavez Family History*, p. 42.

minister had important healing powers and continued bringing family members to attend the Baptist services with him.[10]

For his part, my great-grandfather, Aniceto started to attend Methodist services. He remained a member of that church for the rest of his life and was – when he died in 1946 – his services were held at the Methodist Mexican Mission. Most of my aunts and uncles – including my mother, Bessie – became members of the Baptist Church. Aunt Julia Dominguez and her husband Eleno Salazar had also attended Methodist services but, like Uncle Celestino and Felicitas (Dominguez) Morales, they became involved with the Spanish Church of the Nazarene. Uncle Pablo became a member of Church of God Prophesy organization.

In 1924, according to Uncle Jesse Dominguez, Geronimo started to build a house for his family in the Turner District of Kansas

---

[10] *Ibid.*

City. The new Dominguez residence was located below a hill across from the "ditch." Soon after, however, the Santa Fe Railroad decided that they needed the land that Geronimo had built on, so they destroyed the house to make room for more railroad trackage.[11]

During the 1920s, the Mexican press in Kansas City became very vocal in its opinions about the treatment of Mexican nationals in the area. The Hispanic Press in Kansas started to complain about the Santa Fe Railroads policy towards Mexican workers. *El Cosmopolitia* of Kansas City started to point out that workers earned only $1.125 to $1.50 per day for their ten-to-twelve-hour workday with the Santa Fe. For this reason, *El Cosmopolita* openly encouraged Kansas City Mexicans to work for the Union Pacific or Burlington Railroads instead of the Santa Fe.[12]

---

[11] *Ibid.*, p. 6.

[12] Valerie Marie Mendoza, *The Creation of a Mexican Immigrant Community in Kansas City, 1890-1930*, p. 72; *El Cosmopolita*, April 8, 1916; April 22, 1916; Ted McDaniel (ed.), *Our Land: A History of Lyon County Kansas* (Emporia: Emporia State Press, 1976), p. 162.

The words of the Hispanic press became an important vocal force that the railroads had to contend with. During the late 1920s, the Mexican immigrants were now represented 15.68% of all immigrants to the U.S.[13] By this point, six major railroads were employing between 32,000 and 42,000 Mexican track workers, depending on the season. These laborers comprised 75% of the total track force.[14] Through the efforts of the Mexican-American Press, some grievances were made against offending employers.

As most of my uncles came of age, they started to go to work for the Santa Fe. With so many Spanish-speaking employees, the Atchison, Topeka and Santa Fe Railway Co. even published a Spanish dictionary of track-laying terms to be used by Anglo foremen with their Mexican workers.

---

[13] Judith Fincher Laird, *op. cit.*, p. 66.

[14] Mark Reisler, *By the Sweat of Their Brown: Mexican Immigrant Labor in the United States, 1900-1940* (Westport, Conn.: Greenwood Press, 1976), p. 96.

SECOND-CLASS CITIZENS

The Great Depression

When the Great Depression hit at the beginning of the 1930s, many Mexican-American communities suffered the degradation of repatriation and deportation, even of American-born individuals. For many Mexican laborers around the country, the racial prejudice against them became intolerable and they decided to return to their native states, sometimes scarred and disillusioned by their experiences.

As a result of the massive and indiscriminate raids conducted by U.S. immigration authorities throughout the United States in the early 1930s, more than 400,000 persons were deported back to Mexico. During the peak year of 1931, 138,519 Mexicans were forcefully repatriated.[15]

---

[15] Abraham Hoffman, *Unwanted Mexican Americans in the Great Depression: Repatriation Pressures, 1929-1939* (Tucson: University of Arizona Press, 1974), 174-75.

SECOND-CLASS CITIZENS

In Kansas, the state and local government encouraged the railroads to fire Mexican workers and deport them, even if they had lived in Kansas for decades. But, the Santa Fe Railroad – to their credit – recognized the value of the Mexican laborers even in hard times and made great efforts to keep its work crews. In spite of this, it is believed that the Kansas City Hispanic population shrank to about 2,500 during this decade. Some Mexicans did, in fact, return to Mexico to seek employment in a republic that was now at peace with itself.

Upward mobility came slowly for the Mexican Americans who stayed in Kansas. Their communities remained separated from mainstream society because of the discrimination against them in housing, jobs and education, plus their desire to preserve their own culture. Many uneducated Mexicans and Mexican Americans lacked the training and language skills need to advance beyond low paying positions and stayed mired in the low wages of manual labor jobs.

As with the Dominguez family, many teenage Mexican-American men had to leave school to help support their families. And, in a break with tradition, women often found work outside the home to supplement their incomes. My mother has always related that this period was very difficult for her because it seemed that she was always working. As a young child walking home from school, Anglo children had frequently thrown rocks at her. Because Geronimo needed her to help work the fields and because of the embarrassment and humiliation leveled against her by her classmates, Mother quit school to work at a very young age.

Although my mother's memories of this period are not very good, the Dominguez family neighbor and friend, Esperanza Rangel (now Mrs. Esperanza Amayo) has remembered some good times. As explained earlier, over the last few decades, Esperanza has become an outspoken member of the Kansas City Mexican-American community, a contributor to local newspapers, and an activist for recognition of Mexican-American accomplishments.

SECOND-CLASS CITIZENS

Esperanza was just a little younger than Louie Dominguez, the baby of the family. For the Kansas City Star, she recalled some of her fond memories of these days:[16]

> It seems like only yesterday that we were children, my friends Isabel, Louie and I. In daily ritual we ran across cow pastures and climbed over barbed wire fences on our way to Turner Grade School. Our life was happy and carefree in the '30s and early '40s. Louie was our next-door neighbor on the hill where we lived. Sometimes he would pump water from the well for me. I sensed an awakening attraction, yet meaningful words would be left unspoken, disallowed by time and circumstance.

Esperanza has been interviewed several times by the authors and has vivid memories of her experiences in Turner during the 1930s and 1940s. She remembers Geronimo Dominguez – whom she and the other children in the neighborhood respectfully called "Don" – as a very strict parent. Although the Dominguez family lived as good neighbors upon that hill in Turner, Esperanza does remember one time when Geronimo had an argument with her

---

[16] *Kansas City Times*, June 3, 1984.

parents about the location of the property line between the two homes.

Esperanza smiles as she recalls Geronimo's long green truck with its green canopy. All the families were well aware of the Dominguez family's frequent trips to the beet fields of Nebraska and Colorado. She remembers that the neighborhood children would see that big green truck filled with people returning from Nebraska and everyone would shout, "Here come the Dominguez's." She refers to these outings as "special occasions," because some of their neighbors would also go to work.

Esperanza also remembers the Dominguez family as a very good-looking family. As young Louie grew into adolescence, he developed a square jaw and very handsome features with a gorgeous smile. Louie's older brother Erminio (Minnie) was a tall good looking, well built person but was very quiet.

SECOND-CLASS CITIZENS

Esperanza also had memories of the second youngest in the family. Marshall Dominguez was lighter skinned and slender. He too had the handsome features of a Dominguez and attended school for several years. However, Uncle Marshall eventually became the Dominguez family's second major tragedy, after Luisa's death. On March 27, 1939, Marshall died from acute general nephritis at Mercy Hospital in Kansas City, Missouri. Marshall was only 14 years, 8 months, and 23 days old at the time of his death. My family has always believed that this was a needless death.

In the 1930s, the teachers at the schools in the Kansas City area were very adamant about the use of the Spanish language in school. They told the parents of their students not to speak Spanish at home. To do so might interfere with their English-language education. Uncle Marshall had apparently spoken Spanish at school a few times. It has been said that a certain teacher had physically abused him because of this transgression.

SECOND-CLASS CITIZENS

We have long believed that this abuse led directly or indirectly to his death at such a young age. When my older sisters went to school they had the same teacher and were very wary of the woman.

My Uncle Jesse also started a family during the 1930s. Because he was an older son in the family, Jesse spent a great deal of time going to work in the beet fields in Nebraska, Colorado, North Dakota and Montana. While working in the Mitchell, Nebraska beet fields, Jesse met a young girl named Maria (Mary) Chavez, who had been born on June 14, 1922 in Cheyenne, Wyoming. On March 14, 1935, in Gering, Nebraska, Jesse Lujan Dominguez and Maria Chavez were married in the local courthouse.

The union of Jesse and Mary would be blessed with nine daughters and six sons. By the time of her death on March 3, 2003 (at the age of 79), Aunt Mary had left behind – in addition to her husband and children – a total of 49 grandchildren, 58 great-grandchildren and one great great granddaughter. Louie Gonzales, in his recent works about the Dominguez family, has gone into great detail about the lives and accomplishments of Jesse, Mary and their family.[17]

A prevailing theme in my family's history is their service. My family's service was rendered to relatives, to community, to church, and to their country. The decade of the 1940s and the onset of World War II would sorely test our resolve but, we would persevere through the difficult periods.

---

[17] Louie Gonzales, *The Dominguez – Chavez Family History*, pp. 6, 42-43.

MAKING A LIVING

The Dream and the Reality

Dominguez Family friend, Esperanza Amayo, in writing for the Kansas City Kansan in 1995, explained that "the American Dream is alluring and entices immigrants, legal and illegal, from every corner of earth."[1] And in an interview with the authors, she stated that the Mexican immigrants to Kansas in days of old "arrived in Kansas City with the same passions and aspirations as foreign nationals do today." Esperanza added that many Mexican-American Kansans of her generation "were born here of those immigrants," and it was they who bore the brunt of racial discrimination and segregation that dominated Kansas City for the first half of the Twentieth Century.

But Esperanza is proud to point out that "second-generation Mexican Americans" – a group which includes my parents, uncles and aunts – played important roles "in war and peace to earn a

---

[1] Esperanza Amayo, "Be Proud of Immigrants" [from the "Your View/ Letters to the Readers Column], Kansas City *Kansan*, February 1, 1995.

respectful and dignified place in society." Part of the triumph of Mexican-American determination, according to Esperanza, stems from the fact that native Mexicans came from a nation "where family life is very cohesive" and "parents are highly respected." And, a crucial factor for both her family and her neighbors – the Dominguez family – was religion.[2]

In 1980, Esperanza publicly discussed the endurance of Mexican Americans. In a lengthy letter to the Kansas City *Star*, she wrote about the "blatant discrimination" that Mexican Americans experienced in the silver-smelting community of Argentine. As recently as the 1960s, in fact, Esperanza pointed out that "there was a clearly defined area in Argentine beyond which Mexican-Americans could not live."[3]

---

[2] *Ibid.*

[3] Esperanza Amayo, "Despite Sting of Past Abuse, Mexican-Americans Endure," Kansas City *Star*, November 19, 1980.

MAKING A LIVING

Discrimination in employment remained a serious problem for the entire first half of the Twentieth Century. Esperanza's brother, Solomon Rangel, had started working for the Santa Fe Railroad in 1941, but in those days the only job a Mexican American "could hold was laying track. Mexicans had to eat in a boxcar. Later they had separate lunchrooms and restrooms for Mexicans and other workers."[4]

Esperanza cannot hide her disappointment when she points out the level of discrimination against her people. Mexican Americans could not go to some stores and were not allowed to attend certain schools, including Catholic schools. The theaters in several parts of Kansas City were segregated, with the Mexicans were confined to the left side.[5]

---

[4] *Ibid.*

[5] The education of Mexican Americans in Kansas is described in detail by R. M. Cleary, "The Education of Mexican-Americans in Kansas City, Kansas, 1916-1951," (© 2002-2003) accessed at http://www.kckps.org/disthistory/dist-history/ethnic_history/mexican_american/news_publications/rcleary_mexkck/mexkck_index.htm. [Updated September 12, 2003].

MAKING A LIVING

Even some hamburger joints did not serve Hispanics. When her bother Solomon came home on leave from his World War II duties as an American solder, he walked into a burger joint, proudly wearing his uniform and – to Esperanza's utter disgust – was told to leave.

It takes a certain amount of tenacity to deal with unfair situations and patiently resolve them through time and effort. Mexican Americans in Kansas City were not militant. They were a minority who served their time and did their duty. Some battles were fought but most of the progress we made was through patience, endurance, effort and example. In my own life, my parents Daniel and Bessie Morales taught me these virtues.

Daniel Morales

My father, Daniel Morales, was born in Houston on September 23, 1914 as the son of two recently immigrated parents, Olayo Morales and Juana Luevano. Olayo Morales was from the state of

Aguascalientes and Juana was from Villa Hidalgo, a small town in northern Jalisco close to the border of Aguascalientes. Olayo came from a predominantly indigenous Mexican background. My direct Morales line has been traced back to Indian peasants in Lagos de Moreno, Jalisco. Juana came from Spanish stock. Her most distant Luevano ancestor, Lope Ruiz de Esparza, had immigrated from Pamplona in the Basque country of Northern Spain to Mexico in 1593.[6]

Daniel's spiritual life began a month after he was born on October 21, 1914, when his parents took him to Our Lady of Guadalupe Catholic Church and had him baptized. Six years later, according to the 1920 Federal census, Olayo Morales, a native of Mexico, lived at 304 Walker Street in Houston, Harris County, Texas. Living in Enumeration District 66, Olayo was listed as a 30-year-

---

[6] The Indigenous roots of the Morales family are discussed in length in Donna S. Morales and John P. Schmal, *The Indigenous Roots of a Mexican-American Family* (Bowie, Maryland: Heritage Books, Inc., 2003).

old white male who had immigrated in 1911. His occupation was listed as "driver" of an "express wagon."

Olayo's wife, Juana, was also listed as 30 years old, even though she was actually 35 years of age. The children listed were Carmen (son, 15 years old), Celestino (son, 13 years old), Maria (daughter, 7 years old), and Daniel (son, 5 years old). Maria and Daniel were both born in the United States, while all the other members of the family were natives of Mexico.

During the 1920s, my Morales family heard about the need for Mexican laborers in Mitchell and Scottsbluff, Nebraska. So they decided to go north to take part in the sugar beet harvest. Recruiters in the Houston area had enlisted the services of Olayo and his entire family. Originally, the work was seasonal, but after Olayo died and Juana remarried, the family decided to stay in Kiowa Township.

When the census-taker arrived at their doorstep in 1930, the Morales family had undergone very profound changes. The head of the household was Louis Garcia, the stepfather of Daniel and Juana's second husband. My grandmother, Juana, was listed as "Jenny Garcia," and my father's given name was spelled "Danial." Daniel was fifteen years old at this time and described his occupation as "laborer" on a "beet farm." Daniel's 5-year-old stepsister, Carmen Garcia, also lived in the household. In 1947, Carmen would marry my mother's younger brother, Erminio Dominguez.[7]

Daniel and Bessie

In 1932, Daniel Morales came to Kansas. He first worked for the railroad and was married to one Agripina Llanos. However, that marriage ended very soon when Agripina died in childbirth. Soon after he met Bessie Dominguez who – like him – was a native of

---

[7] The census schedules containing the Morales family in Scotts Bluff County, Nebraska can be found on Microfilm Roll T626_1293, Nebraska, Enumeration District 18, Page 11B.

Texas and the child of Mexican immigrants. Bessie (Pabla) Dominguez was a beautiful woman with very exotic Indian features, an inheritance of her ancestors who spent many centuries working the mines in northern Zacatecas.

On April 18, 1937, after a short courtship, Daniel and Bessie were married in Jackson County, Missouri. Over the years, Daniel and Bessie would have a total of eight daughters: Jenny, Olivia, Mary Ellen, Eleanor, Ruth, Carol, Donna, and Abigail. I was the sixth daughter out of the eight children.

Life In Kansas

Daniel and Bessie were both very attractive people. On the following page, we have reproduced a picture taken of my parents soon after they were married.

Daniel and Bessie Morales, circa 1939

Soon after he was married, my father found a job as a laborer for the Santa Fe Railroad. The Santa Fe was still a major employer of Mexican Americans in Kansas City, and many members of my mother's family had been employed by the Santa Fe over the previous two decades. In these early years, my parents lived in a small place at 1015 South 24th Street. As the Great Depression gripped our nation during the late 1930s, my father struggled to make a living and feed a small family at the same time.

When World War II began with the attack on Pearl Harbor in December 1941, my father decided that he must serve his country and enlist in the Army. However, my mother was adamantly opposed to such a move and made her feelings about that very clear to him. With two daughters and a wife to feed, Daniel had too many responsibilities and, in the end, he decided not to enlist.

However, as the American economy shifted to a war footing, Daniel did find a way to contribute to the Allied war effort. Soon after Pearl Harbor, my father started a new job at the Kansas City Structural Steel Company and moved his small family to 820 South 6th Street. Daniel's employer fabricated much of the steel for the buildings that were constructed in the Kansas City area.

However, when World War II started, many private industries were asked to contribute to the common war effort. As a result, Kansas City Structural Steel Company was given the responsibility of building hundreds of landing craft barges for the United States Navy.[8]

As the war progressed and Allied victory seemed likely, Daniel started to look for other jobs to support his ever-growing family. First, he became a clerk for the C.R.I.&P Railroad (Chicago and

---

[8] Source: "Kansas City War Contribution," Online: <http://www.geocities.com/kcghostsquadron/CAF-KC-History.html>. November 27, 2002. Copyright 1996-2002 Commemorative Air Force, Inc.

Rock Island Railroad). Almost simultaneously, he started working as a waiter at the Muelbach Hotel in Kansas City. Father also took a great interest in theology. Because he was a religious man, he decided to become a Sunday school teacher at the First Mexican American Baptist Church in Kansas City. Daniel would teach Sunday school for four decades.

Bessie Dominguez Morales' life as a mother was never easy. She had to take care of all the children and, at the same time, she had to go to work to provide financial support for the family. More than anyone else, my mother taught me about endurance. When I was a child, she spent years working for farmers in the Kansas City area.

As a matter of fact, when I was just a small girl, farming became a family endeavor. Mother and Father would take me and my sisters to work for a farmer named Billie. On these frequent outings, I would bring along a basket and help my family with the harvest. This family effort was an important event. It was an opportunity to learn about responsibility and to become knowledgeable about farming. Many Mexican-American families like mine depended greatly upon farming as a means of putting food on the table and as an opportunity to make some extra money.

For me and each of my sisters, our allowance from this family outing to Billie's farm was a Godsend. With the money I made, I had lunch money and I bought supplies for school. In the 1950s, a small amount of money could go a long way because I was also able to buy shoes and materials for clothing. Mother taught me how to sew so that I could make my own clothes. This period of my life made me the person I am today.

My father had an enormous amount of energy and a great enthusiasm for life and service. In 1975, he retired from his job at the Rock Island Railroad. In the 1990s, he became increasingly frail with stomach problems. He was diagnosed with stomach cancer and passed away on November 16, 1996 at Trinity Lutheran Manor. His funeral was held on Tuesday, November 19 at Simmons Funeral Home, followed by burial at Maple Hill Cemetery. At the time of his death, my father left behind his wife, eight children, 16 grandchildren and 16 great-grandchildren.

A DISTINGUISHED MILITARY RECORD

Pearl Harbor

My family is a patriotic family and, like many other American families, we have been willing to make great sacrifices for this country. World War II became a great test of my family's loyalty to America, but – in our eyes – there was never any question about where we stood on the issue of patriotism or what we had to do. As Americans, the answers were very clear right from the very start.

On the afternoon of December 7, 1941, my grandfather Geronimo Dominguez returned to his home in Turner from church and family socializing with his three children who still lived at home: 21-year-old Effie, 19-year-old Erminio and 15-year-old Louie. After turning on the radio, the Dominguez family heard the startling news: The Japanese Imperial Navy had launched a surprise attack on the American naval fleet at Pearl Harbor, killing 2,235 servicemen and sixty civilians. Equally devastating was the fact that our entire Hawaii fleet, sitting at anchor in the harbor, was destroyed. Simultaneously, the Japanese launched military strikes throughout Southeast Asia, including invasions of the Philippine Islands (an American colony), Singapore, Malaysia, and the Dutch East Indies.

Geronimo, by now, suffered from tuberculosis and a chronic cough. Although he was only fifty-seven years old, he was not a well man. With the startling news, the Dominguez children fell into a state of shock and did not fully comprehend what this could mean for them or for the country. But, as the reality sank in, both Erminio and Louie started to express anger and outrage over this surprise attack. "How the could the Japanese do this to us," Erminio asked, what would make them thing they could get away with it?"

The whole family listened when President Franklin Delano Roosevelt made his famous speech to the American people, decrying the savage assault on American territory. The

A DISTINGUISHED MILITARY RECORD

President's opening words – "Yesterday, December 7, 1941 - a date which will live in infamy - the United States of America was suddenly and deliberately attacked by naval and air forces of the Empire of Japan." Mr. Roosevelt pointed out that the Japanese and American governments had been having conversations "toward the maintenance of peace in the Pacific." But all Japan's peaceful gestures, it now appeared, had been feigned to lull the United States into a false sense of security. On December 8, the U.S. Congress – acting on the request of the President – declared war on Japan.

In Berlin on December 8, 1941, the German dictator Adolph Hitler was elated, stating to his Propaganda Minister, Josef Goebbels, that "we have ally that has not been defeated in 1,500 years!" Soon after, on December 11, Germany and Italy – the two primary Axis Powers of Europe – declared war on the United States. What the Axis Powers did not realize at the time is that, instead of crippling an enemy and rendering him ineffective, they had awakened a sleeping giant, the United States of America.

Once he had received the news about the actions of Germany and Italy, President Roosevelt addressed the American people, explaining that "the long-known and the long-expected has thus taken place. The forces endeavoring to enslave the entire world now are moving toward this hemisphere. Never before has there been a greater challenge to life, liberty and civilization." Once again at Roosevelt's request, the United States Congress declared war, this time against Germany and Italy.

In a mere five days, America had gone from a nation at peace to a nation at war with three formidable enemies, Germany, Italy and Japan. Our nation and our armed forces were now in a very vulnerable position. In December 1941, our armed forces could not have mounted an effective resistance to the Japanese incursions taking place throughout the Pacific region.

A DISTINGUISHED MILITARY RECORD

But the American people never considered surrender or compromise. Able-bodied men in every town of every state made painful decisions to leave their families behind to defend their nation in its time of need. Likewise, many women went to work in factories and plants that would create the weapons we needed to win the war. On May 14th 1942, a newly enacted law created the Women's Army Auxiliary Corps, permitting women the additional opportunity to serve in the American armed forces.

Many Americans do not realize the severity of our situation when we went to war in December 1941. And many do not realize that the war had actually started long before the attack on Pearl Harbor. When World War II started on September 1, 1939, with the German invasion of Poland, the United States declared its neutrality. In fact, the U.S. was not an active participant in the war between September 1939 and December 7, 1941 – a period of two years and three months.

A DISTINGUISHED MILITARY RECORD

During the first two years of World War II, from September 1939 through December 1941, a series of startling military victories permitted German domination of the European continent. After the conquest of Poland in 1939, Adolph Hitler gave the order to invade other countries, even while professing his desire to make peace with Great Britain and France. Using Blitzkrieg (Lightning-war) tactics, the German military had overwhelmed and destroyed the armies of France, Poland, Norway, Yugoslavia, and Greece. In addition, Denmark, Belgium, Luxembourg, and the Netherlands had been occupied after short campaigns. Hitler had been able to achieve his conquests, partly through the help of his allies, Italy, Rumania, Hungary, and Bulgaria.

On June 22, 1941, Nazi Germany – with the help of her allies, Romania, Hungary and Finland – launched a massive invasion across a battle line that stretched almost 2,000 miles from the Black Sea to the Arctic Ocean. Between July and early December 1941, German troops conquered the Baltic States (Estonia,

Lithuania and Latvia) and large tracts of Russian territory, including most of the Ukraine and Byelorussia.

In order to give the reader an understanding of the grave situation in the European Theater during 1942, we have created a map on the following page, which will show the reader the amount of territory occupied by the Axis Powers in August 1942.[1] The pre-war boundaries of Europe (1939) have been indicated, while gray shading indicates the occupied territory as of August 1942. However, the Allied gains from November 1942 to June 1944 whittled away at Hitler's empire, and the boundaries of the Axis Empire are also indicated for June 1944.

---

[1] Title: "World War II: The European Theater (1942-1944)." © Copyright 2003, Eddie Martinez and John Schmal.

© Copyright 2003, Eddie Martinez and John Schmal

World War II: The European Theater (1942-1944)

A DISTINGUISHED MILITARY RECORD

As our map clearly delineates, in August 1942, the Germans controlled large portions of Russian territory. They had surrounded Moscow, the Soviet capital, in late 1941 but never actually took the famous city. The Battle of Stalingrad – lasting from September 1942 to February 1943 – would soon turn the tide against the Germans.

By June 1944, Allied forces had taken all of Northern Africa and southern Italy from the Axis Powers. But most important of all was the June 6th D-Day invasion of Normandy in northwestern France that would eventually bring Allied forces within striking distance of Germany.

Erminio Dominguez

It was during America's darkest hours that 20-year-old Erminio Dominguez enlisted in the armed forces. Uncle Erminio joined the military on September 2, 1942 at a time when American forces were battling the Japanese on the small island of Guadalcanal, some 5399 kilometers (3355 miles) from Tokyo. Most Americans had no illusions that it would be a long road to Tokyo and victory. At the same time, half a world away, German forces ruled over most of the continent of Europe.

Most of the neutral countries were carefully avoiding confrontation with Germany, while the fighting on the Russian front, seemed to be far away. In May 1942, Allied military planners were planning a major landing in North Africa to attack German, Italian and Vichy French forces, but this attack would not take place until many months later, in November.

Uncle Erminio's military assignment was with the 2nd Squadron of the 102nd Cavalry Regiment, part of which would later be designated as the 117th Cavalry Reconnaissance Squadron (Mechanized). This unit had been formed in large part from the New Jersey National Guards' "Essex Troop." In November 1940, the War Department had selected seven National Guard and two regular Army Cavalry Regiments to be reorganized as "Horse-Mechanized Cavalry." With a National Emergency expected in the months to come, the "Essex Troop" was one of the units honored to be selected for this mobilization. On January 6, 1941 – almost a year before Pearl Harbor – the Essex Troop was inducted into federal service. Then, on April 6, 1942, the Essex Troop was officially reorganized as the 102d Cavalry Regiment (Horse/Mechanized) at Newark, New Jersey. From here, the Regiment was sent to Fort Jackson, South Carolina to start training for overseas duty. With this transformation, the Regiment went from a peacetime strength of 500 men to 1,500 men, following the recruitment of new soldiers, including Erminio Dominguez.

In September 1942, after a period of intense training in the United States, the 102nd Cavalry Regiment prepared to depart for overseas duty. During these dark days, the Atlantic Ocean represented a dangerous obstacle. The German U-boat Campaign was being waged in the Atlantic with great success. In August 1942, German

U-boats had succeeded in sinking two million tons of shipping, both military and civilian.

However, Uncle Erminio and the 2nd Squadron successfully crossed the Atlantic and arrived in Liverpool, England. For a short time, the Squadron was housed in the Village of Fairford, where training was continued in order to keep the troops in a high state of proficiency.[2] In the meantime, a massive Allied invasion – consisting of 107,000 British and American forces – invaded North Africa. Allied forces – delivered to their destination by a fleet of 300 ships – landed at Casablanca (Morocco), Oran (Algeria) and Algiers (Algeria), which had been under the control of Vichy French forces. Although Algiers lay 1,928 kilometers (1,198 miles) from Berlin, these landings represented a significant

---

[2] Harold J. Samsel, *The Operational History of the 117th Cavalry Reconnaissance Squadron (Mecz.), World War II* (Westfield, New Jersey: 117th Cavalry Association, 1982), "Chapter III: Preparation for Overseas Duty, 1942," pp. 28-29.

threat to Germany's hold over Europe. But, once again, the road to Berlin and victory would be a long one.

Assignment to Security Command

In December 1942, the 2nd Squadron was officially detached from the 102nd Regiment for a special assignment with the Security Command. The Squadron was temporarily housed at the Shrivingham Barracks in Swindon. Then, on December 24, 1942, the Squadron set sail from Glasgow, Scotland for an unknown destination. The uncertainty the troops felt was relieved when, on January 3, 1943, 2nd Squadron entered the Algiers Harbor.[3]

At the moment, heavy fighting was taking place in Tunisia, where German and Italian troops desperately tried to maintain Axis control over North Africa. The German resistance continued for many months, but gradually the Allied forces were able to push them into a corner of Tunisia. Then, in May 1943, the Allies

---

[3] *Ibid.*, pp. 33-35.

forced the surrender of more than 250,000 German and Italian troops, effectively removing the Axis Powers from the African continent.

To their surprise, the 2nd Squadron was not sent to the battlefield. Instead of going into combat, the Squadron was assigned to the Security Command of Allied Force Headquarters. In this capacity, they became the primary combat security force for Headquarters and its associated installations. But, most important of all, the Squadron was ordered to provide personal protection for General Dwight D. Eisenhower. During their stay in Algeria, the men of the 2nd Squadron were housed in the small town of Douera, 29 kilometers (18 miles) south of Algiers and nearly 646 kilometers (400 miles) from the front lines.[4]

---

[4] *Ibid,* "Chapter IV: North Africa, 1943," pp. 36, 38.

A DISTINGUISHED MILITARY RECORD

The strength of the Second Squadron was now 34 officers and 673 enlisted men, including my uncle, Erminio Dominguez. It wasn't long before the men of the 2nd Squadron would be called into action. On January 17, 1943, they came into contact with German parachutists who had landed near Palestro, 40 kilometers (25 miles) southeast of Algiers. Having responded with full force, the Squadron eliminated the enemy threat very quickly. Around the same time, some elements of the 2nd Squadron were assigned to protect General Eisenhower's Forward Command Post at Constantine, Tunisia. For the next few months, the Squadron would also spend a great deal of time training Free French soldiers in the art of war.[5]

In May 1943, the Germans and Italians lost their foothold in Northern Africa. With this success, the Allies were determined to keep the pressure on the Axis troops. On July 10, 1943, an amphibious force of 3,000 ships and landing craft brought eight

---

[5] *Ibid.*, p. 40.

divisions of men – 160,000 soldiers in all – to the shores of Sicily. Although the fighting in Sicily was fierce at times, the operation was completed by August 17, 1943. Not long after (September 3), British and American forces crossed the Straits of Messina to invade Italy, marking their first appearance on the shores of continental Europe.

A Soldier In Training

Back in Kansas City, on April 13, 1943, Geronimo Dominguez passed away at his home in Turner, Kansas. For the last year of his life, Geronimo had been suffering from pulmonary tuberculosis. He had grown steadily weaker and sicker over the years. At the time of his death, Geronimo was survived by four daughters (Felicitas Morales, Juliana Salazar, Bessie Morales, and Effie Dominguez) and by four sons (Pablo, Jesse, Erminio, and Louis). Geronimo was also survived by his father, Aniceto

---

A DISTINGUISHED MILITARY RECORD

Dominguez, his brother Ned Dominguez and his half-sister, Carlota Dominguez Calzado.

While most of Geronimo's children were now married, his youngest son Louie was living at home and attending Turner High School. Young Louie had watched the progress of the war with great interest. He was intrigued and fascinated by the image of soldiers marching off to war to save America from the Fascist threat. Louie admired and emulated his older brother, Erminio, and aspired to be like him. He could not wait for the opportunity to become a soldier and wear his own uniform.

In his letters to Erminio, Louie expressed a great desire to enlist in the armed services so that he might take part in this great struggle against tyranny. But he was still too young to enlist on his own. Because he was still a minor, Louie pleaded with his brothers and sisters in Kansas City to give their approval for him to become a soldier. But the family remained adamant and would not sign for him. Erminio said that he would support Louie's joining the military, but he was half a world away and could not take part in the discussions with the other family members.

Meanwhile, overseas, on November 30, 1943, the 2nd Squadron severed all its connections with the 102nd Cavalry Regiment (which was still stationed in England). The 2nd Squadron was now redesignated as the "117th Cavalry Reconnaissance Squadron Mechanized."[6] The unit's first assignment in December 1943 was to leave their position and march a thousand miles west to the Moroccan city of Marrakech, where they would protect the life of British Prime Minister, Winston Churchill, as he arrived in North Africa.[7]

There had been major concerns about a German attempt to kidnap Churchill. On September 12, 1943, a German airborne unit had

---

[6] *Ibid.,* "The Long Desert Year, 1943: North Africa," p. 47.

[7] *Ibid.*, pp. 47-49.

engineered the successful rescue of the Italian dictator, Benito Mussolini. Although there was no direct evidence that the Germans were planning such a mission against Churchill, the British and Americans wanted to take no chances. On January 15, 1944, Prime Minister Churchill returned to England, and the 117th Cavalry's latest mission came to an end.[8]

The Italian Campaign

In April 1944, the 117th Cavalry Reconnaissance Squadron was assigned to the 5th Army of General Mark Clark, which was making its way up the Italian Peninsula, against stiff German resistance. After a year and a half of special security assignments, Uncle Erminio's unit was finally going to go into front-line action in the Italian campaign. On May 22, the 117th went into action at Itri and Sperlonga, which were both about a hundred miles south of Rome.

---

[8] *Ibid.*, "Chapter V: North African Operations, 1944," pp. 50-53.

A DISTINGUISHED MILITARY RECORD

The Allied forces steadily drove the enemy northward toward the Eternal City, and on June 4, 1944, advance patrols of the 3rd Division had reached the outer limits of Rome. By the morning of June 5th, all elements on the 117th had made their way into Rome. In a mere twelve days, the 117th Squadron had advanced almost 161 kilometers (100 miles).

Delirious with joy and happiness, millions of Italians welcomed the liberators with great fanfare. Italians throughout Rome climbed onto American tanks and armored cars to greet the soldiers. On the following day, many members of the 117th Cavalry attended Mass in St. Peter's Cathedral as the Pope, assisted by thirty-four cardinals, celebrated a Mass of Liberation. The Pope, speaking in English, expressed the heartfelt thanks of the entire Italian people to the Allied troops that had freed Rome from Nazi occupation.[9]

---

[9] *Ibid.*, "Chapter VI: The Italian Campaign, 1944," pp. 63-65.

A DISTINGUISHED MILITARY RECORD

Reflecting on the reception that the Americans received from the Romans, unit historian Colonel Harold J. Samsel wrote, "All the hardships and loneliness of a soldier seemed well worth whatever sacrifices have been made. The Italian people suffered badly under the Germans... To see the extreme happiness on their faces as we liberated their lands made one proud to be wearing an American Uniform. Without a doubt, we all gained great moral strength and justification for our cause."[10]

After the fall of Rome, the 117th Regiment was ordered to continue its journey northward. However, according to Colonel Samsel, "the remainder of June saw the 117th engaged in heavy fighting north of Rome, in almost constant contact with the enemy." Colonel Samsel explains that "fire fights were frequent and deadly, artillery fire was heavy, and the German anti-tank guns

---

[10] *Ibid.*, p. 65.

and mines took their toll. Casualties were high, for the enemy was making the Fifth Army fight for every foot of ground it gave up."[11]

On June 29, 1944, the 117th Reconnaissance Squadron was relieved of its mission on the Italian front and was ordered to proceed to Naples, where it was then reassigned to the VI Corps as part of the 7th Army's "Operation Anvil" (the Allied amphibious invasion of Southern France). Earlier in the month, Allied forces had landed on the shores of Normandy in northwestern France. However, after some initial successes, it appeared that the Allied forces were pinned down by strong German resistance. Some military planners believed that an invasion of Southern France might cause the Germans to divert some of their forces south, thus giving the Allied forces in Normandy some breathing room.

---

[11] *Ibid.*, "Into Combat: Liberation of the Eternal City," pp. 12-13.

A DISTINGUISHED MILITARY RECORD

Operation Anvil

On August 14, 1944, the invasion convoy set sail and on August 15th, the Allied forces made a successful landing in Southern France between Toulon and Cannes. The 117th Squadron was now reassigned as a reconnaissance element of "Task Force Butler," commanded by Brigadier General F. B. Butler.

The activities of the Squadron from August 15 to September 1 have been described in detail by Colonel Harold J. Samsel in *The Operational History of the 117th Reconnaissance Squadron (Mecz.), World War II.* Task Force Butler had been ordered to cut off the retreat of the German 19th Army that was moving northward to escape the Allied onslaught. In four days, the 117th Squadron advanced 306 kilometers (190 miles) from the beachhead, liberating 6,645 square miles of French territory and capturing more than 2,500 prisoners. For this service, the Squadron was later awarded the Croix de Guerre by the French Government.

On August 30, 1944, the 117th Squadron was relieved of its attachment to Task Force Butler and reattached to the VI Corps. They were now 442 kilometers (275 miles) from their original beachhead on the shores of the Mediterranean. The Squadron had successfully harassed the German 19th Army as it retreated toward Germany. In the words of Colonel Samsel, the American forces "kept stabbing at the flanks of the German Army fastly retreating to Germany."[12]

Montrevel

At the beginning of September, the 117th Squadron received a new assignment that would dramatically alter the destinies of all the unit's men, including my uncle, Erminio Dominguez. On September 2, 1944, the unit had received the following message from Brigadier General Carlton, the Deputy Commander of the 6th Corps: "Seize and hold Montrevel by daylight, establish road

---

[12] *Ibid.,* "Chapter VII: The Campaign in France, 1944: Part 3. Action at Montrevel, France," p. 114.

blocks on the roads leading into the town from the South, the East and the North so as to cut off the escape route of the 19th Germany Army."[13]

Troop B, commanded by Captain John L. Wood, was to lead the attack on Montrevel and Troop A, commanded by Thomas C. Piddington, was to keep the lines of communication open. Initially, the seizure of Montrevel went well, and the Americans were able to capture seventy-five German prisoners. However, the American seizure of Montrevel had cut off the main supply route of the 11th Panzer Division, which was engaged at Borg with the American 45th Infantry Division, some distance to the south.[14]

When General Wend von Wietersheim, the commander of the 11th Panzer Division, found out about the seizure of Montrevel, he sent

---

[13] *Ibid.*, p. 115-1; Harold J. Samsel, *The Battle of Montrevel, France, September 3, 1944: 117th CavalryReconnaissance Squadron (Mechanized)*. (Princeton, New Jersey: Triangle Reproduction, 1986, 2nd edition).

[14] *Ibid.*

a reconnaissance battalion, reinforced by six tanks and an engineer battalion, to recapture the town. Seeking to cover its own retreat route, the 11th Panzer Division surrounded Montrevel and pinched off the escape routes in and out of the town. Quickly, the Germans moved into Montrevel to extinguish all resistance and safeguard their supply routes.

According to the Departmental Records Branch of the Army's Adjutant General's Office, "again and again, the Troops [of the 117th Regiment] launched attacks against the greatly superior armor and numerical superiority of the enemy. These forays kept the enemy forces off balance and in the dark as to the strength of the defenders."[15]

Erminio Dominguez and the other men of 117th Regiment were able to inflict heavy losses on the German forces. However, the

---

[15] Departmental Records Branch, Department of Army, The Adjutant General's Office, Opn. Rpt., 117th Cavalry Recn. Sq. (M), September 1944.

vastly superior German forces, with three years of experience on the Russian front, used heavy artillery against the defenders and gradually squeezed the American defenders into a small corner of the town. As the day war on and the fighting became more intense, the American casualties mounted steadily, while their ammunition ran low.

Finally, according to one battle account, "the handful of [surviving] Americans, surrounded, exhausted, their ammunition expended, with five killed, 60 wounded, 70 prisoners of war, most of their equipment and vehicles in flames, had no choice." By the end of that day, September 3, 1944, the beleaguered Americans of the 117th Cavalry Regiment in Montrevel surrendered to the German forces.[16]

The Battle of Montrevel provoked controversy over the years. Some analysts, including Colonel Samsel, felt that VI Corps had

---

[16] *Ibid.,* Sub-Event #5.

assigned this mission "without the full infantry and tank support so vitally essential when opposing an enemy force led by an outstanding armored division." Colonel Samsel later wrote that the military commanders had not anticipated the powerful reaction of the Germans, who "reacted violently and attacked in strength" with their "most capable troops."

The gallant men of the 117th who defended Montrevel – including my Uncle Erminio – were praised for their bravery and tenacity, even by their adversaries. The Adjutant General's report stated that "the aggressive tactics and the personal bravery of the Troops within the town were of such a high degree that the enemy commander displayed considerable amazement that the force which had opposed him was so small numerically and so lacking in heavy armor."

A DISTINGUISHED MILITARY RECORD

Prisoner of War

By the end of the day, the German 11th Panzer Division had captured all the surviving soldiers of the 117th Squadron. Many soldiers from both Troop A and Troop B were captured, including Private Erminio Dominguez. The prisoners of war were quickly transported by train to Stalag VII-A at Moosburg in the German state of Bavaria.

The POW camp at Moosburg was established in September 1939 as Kriegsgefangenen-Mannschafts-Stammlager, just a short distance north of the city by the same name and 35 kilometers (22 miles) northeast of Munich. Originally, the camp was built for the purpose of housing some 14,000 French prisoners. But, by the end of the war in 1945, more than 80,000 Allied soldiers had been interned in the camp.[17] As the Allies made their way into German territory in March 1945, the German military started to transfer

---

[17] "Moosburg Online: POW Camp Stalag VII A." Online: <http://www.stalag.moosburg.org>. [Last update: May 23, 2003].

POWs from other camps to Moosburg, leading to a serious case of overcrowding.

From early September 1944 to April 29, 1945 – a total of eight months – Erminio Dominguez was an inmate of this prisoner of war camp. Although the Allies still had a great deal of fighting to do, Uncle Erminio would not be involved any more battles for the duration of the war.

IN THE SERVICE OF HIS COUNTRY

The Landings In Normandy

The United States entered World War II in December 1941. For the next three years and five months, American forces would be engaged in battle against German, Italian and Japanese forces until Germany's surrender on May 8, 1945. The war with Japan would last a few months longer – for three years and nine months – until Japan's surrender on September 2, 1945. Many battles were fought during this period, but the D-Day Invasion of the Normandy coastline (in France), starting on June 6, 1944 was a pivotal event in the hostilities against the Germans, probably second only in importance to the Russian victory over the Germans at Stalingrad, after a six-month battle from August 1942 to February 1943.

During the first six months of 1944, the United States and Great Britain had concentrated an enormous amount of land, naval, and air forces in England to prepare for Operation Overlord, the Allied assault on Hitler's "Fortress Europe." The Allies employed more than 12,000 fighters and bombers against German defenses in France and Germany, in an attempt to weaken the German resolve. The air forces bombed railways, attacked German industrial centers and tried to isolate Axis forces on the battlefield.

Finally, on June 6, 1944, the largest armada ever assembled reached the shores of Normandy. In the great amphibious operation of the Twentieth Century, 3,000 landing craft, 2,500 other ships and 500 naval vessels – as well as 822 aircraft – delivered 154,000 British, Canadian, and American soldiers to the shores of Normandy. By the end of that day, Hitler's Atlantic Wall had been breached and the Allies struggled to increase their foothold in France. The Allies suffered 9,500 casualties that day, while the Germans probably lost a slightly smaller number of soldiers.

But the landings at Normandy were only the beginning of the end for Hitler. The Allies made slow progress in expanding their beachheads, and supplies and reinforcements were not coming ashore as rapidly as they had hoped for. A great deal was yet to be done, and America was continuing to send more boys off to war.

Kansas City At War

In 1944, Kansas City was located more than 7,000 kilometers (4,350 miles) from the battlefields of Normandy. But distance from the front line meant little to the citizens of Kansas City. Many civilians in Kansas City played a very important role in the war effort by working in the defense industry. Between December 1941 and August 1945, more than 50,000 employees at North American Aviation's Fairfax Plant in Kansas City, Kansas built 6,608 B-25 Mitchell medium bombers, which – because of its versatility – was used in every theater of the war.[1] The Darby Company – also located in the Fairfax District – was a major producer of boilermakers and steel fabricators.

---

[1] Scott O'Kelley, "Winning the Home Front," UMKC University Libraries (2001-2002). Online: <http://www.umkc.edu/lib/spec-col/ww2/PacificTheater/home_front_txt.htm>. [Last Updated May 9, 2002].

IN THE SERVICE OF HIS COUNTRY

The work of the men and women in the defense industries were an integral part of America's World War II effort, and the defense industry in Kansas was one of the most important urban contributors to this cause. However, enlisting men in the armed forces was the primary goal of Uncle Sam. Men were dying at the front lines and these soldiers had to be replaced by new soldiers on a regular basis. It is believed that some 215,000 Kansans served in uniform during World War II, and that 3,500 were killed in action between 1941 and 1945.

Seventeen-year-old Louie Dominguez – a few days away from graduation from Turner High School – paid careful attention to the news from the Normandy battlefields. He wanted desperately to become a soldier like his older brother Erminio and wanted to do all that he could to prepare himself for this mission. Louie talked incessantly to his friends and family about his intention to become a soldier. Already, several young Mexican Americans from the Turner District had joined the service and Louie looked forward to joining their ranks and feeling the pride that one gets when he is fighting for an important cause.

Because he was still a minor in the eyes of the law, Louie pleaded with his siblings to approve his entry into the armed forces. And although Erminio was willing to sign for him, the family in Kansas City tried to discourage him. He was, after all, the baby of the family. While Grandpa Aniceto and other Dominguez's felt pride in having Erminio serving their country, they believed that Louie was too young to go to war and possibly risk death at the hands of a fierce and desperate enemy that was being pushed into a corner.

On July 20, 1944, it was learned that dozens of generals took part in an attempted coup d'etat against Hitler. A bomb had exploded in Hitler's map room and several generals were killed. However, Hitler himself survived the blast and was able to take action against the plotters. In the months to come, more than a thousand

German officers and other plotters would be executed, and Hitler continued to wage his war.

Answering Uncle Sam's Call

Finally, July 30th arrived, and Louie Dominguez was eighteen years old. Louie celebrated his birthday by going to Missouri and enlisting in the army almost immediately. Then, on August 15, 1944, Louie Dominguez followed his dream and reported for basic training at Fort McClellan in Alabama. Esperanza Rangel (now Mrs. Esperanza Amayo), Louie's neighbor and friend, soon learned about Louie's enlistment.

In a telephone interview with the authors, Esperanza fondly remembers that her life in Turner seemed so simple during the 1930s and the early 1940s. She and Louie had both attended Turner Grade School, and Louie had later gone on to Turner High School. Now a major world war loomed over the lives of the Mexican American families on the hill in Turner. Esperanza's brothers, Solomon and Tony Rangel, had already gone to war, as did another neighbor, Isaiah Zamarripa, who became an officer in the Army-Air Force. These men and Louie's older brother Erminio became role models for the young and impressionable Louie. Altogether, the ten Mexican-American families on the hill would contribute five soldiers to the war effort, including both Louie and Erminio.

Because they were neighbors, Louie and Esperanza would both go to draw water from the same water pump outside. With delight, Esperanza recalls that whenever she went outside to fetch water, Louie would frequently come out at the same time and help her pump the water. She told the authors that she and Louie had developed an attraction for each other and that, from his house, Louie may have watched for her daily journeys to the water pump. She recalls "I sensed an awakening attraction, yet meaningful words were left unspoken and disallowed by both time and circumstance."

IN THE SERVICE OF HIS COUNTRY

Commenting on the last time she saw Louie, Esperanza told the authors, "Louie looked so fine in his Army uniform as he strode across the dirt road on the hill in Turner." After he had joined the Army, Louie had developed a new walk. When he wore his uniform, Louie now walked with a determined and purposeful gait, exuding both confidence and pride in his new career. Already a handsome young man, Esperanza said that young Louie cut a dashing and impressive figure as he prepared to go overseas.

Esperanza believes that this walk reflected his enthusiasm for his new career and his important mission. For a young boy from a poor Mexican-American family in Turner, the armed services represented a step up in life. Reflecting on her last meeting with Louie, Esperanza wrote "He went to war radiating youthful and patriotic eagerness."[2] On the following page, we have reproduced a photograph of Private Louis Dominguez of the 75th Infantry Division as he appeared in 1944.

---

[2] Kansas City *Star*, June 3, 1984.

Pfc. Louis Dominguez, 1944

IN THE SERVICE OF HIS COUNTRY

A month after his enlistment, Louie and the rest of the Dominguez family were informed by the military that Erminio Dominguez was missing in action on the French front. It would be a couple of weeks before they learned that Erminio had actually survived the Battle of Montrevel and was now a prisoner of war in a German POW camp. This startling information greatly upset young Louie, who was now engaged in his basic training at Fort McClellan. It was a difficult period for Louie, who had looked up to and emulated his older brother.

Learning that his hero and role model had been captured had a dramatic effect on the young teenager. Enraged that the Germans were still capable of mounting such counterattacks and fearing for his brother's life, Louie's patriotic fervor reached a fever pitch. Writing from Fort McClellan, Louie promised his family in Kansas that he would finish his basic training and – with great enthusiasm – take part in the defeat of Nazi Germany, with high hopes that his brother would one day be a free man again. Louie had come to recognize that this war was – for him – a special mission, both to serve his country and to help liberate his brother from German captivity.

After finishing basic training, Louie was attached to the 75th Infantry Division and soon found himself traveling across the Atlantic Ocean on his way to the war zone. In late November 1944, the 75th Infantry Division arrived in England. After a brief training program in Scotland and England, Louie and the other men of the 75th landed at Le Havre, France in mid-December.

The Battle of the Bulge

By the end of 1944, Germany was very clearly losing this war. Allied troops had pushed up to the German border in some areas, while the Russians were making steady gains along the long eastern front. In the meantime, American and British bombs devastated many German cities with intensive bombing. And, in the south, most of the Italian peninsula had fallen into Allied hands.

But, Hitler had one more ace up his sleeve. On December 16,1944, eight German armored divisions and thirteen infantry divisions launched an all-out attack on five divisions of the United States in the Ardennes area of Belgium, Luxembourg and France. Initially, the Ardennes offensive – more popularly known as the "Battle of the Bulge – caught the Allies off guard and pushed back several American divisions.

With this sudden threat looming over the Western Front, the Allied Command quickly rushed the 75th Infantry Division up to the front lines, which they reached just before Christmas. Uncle Louie belonged to the 2nd Platoon of "A Company" (Able Company) of the 289th Infantry Regiment. Able Company saw their first action on Christmas Day, near the town of Erezec in Belgium. Then, on the 27th, the Germans stormed the positions of

A Company, yelling "Give up, it's your last chance." Their attack was met by a "withering wall of fire" that ended the attack.[3]

Sergeant Franklin C. MacCarrick, Jr., the author of the Able Company diary, described the difficulties of fighting a fierce enemy in the dead of winter: "During these days, while morale ran surprisingly high, life was sheer misery. Drenched with icy sleet and rain, sleeping in the open and fighting one's way through the snow-laden trees...provided the men of this company with a picture of the terrors and futility of war that they would never forget. During this time the company strength went steadily downward. Frozen limbs, trench foot, G.I.'s, swollen arms and feet accounted for many of the men who had so far dodged the German ammunition that came their way."[4]

---

[3] Franklin C. MacCarrick, Jr., *Up Front With the Able Doughboys, 289th Infantry: History of Able Company* (August 1945), pp. 1-3. The diary of A Company was graciously donated by Jacque Stoltz (a veteran of the 4th platoon) and by Steven Graber. We owe a debt of gratitude for their cooperation.

[4] *Ibid.*, p. 6.

IN THE SERVICE OF HIS COUNTRY

The 75th Infantry Division – because of its recent arrival and its young, new recruits – was originally dubbed as the "Diaper Division." But the division earned the respect of the other units because of its distinguished record during the Ardennes battle and some observers started to call them the "Bulge Busters."

During the period December 24, 1944 and January 24, 1945, the 75th Infantry Division played a pivotal role in turning back the German offensive, but their losses were heavy: 407 killed, 1,707 wounded, and 334 missing. Another serious problem affecting the men of the 75th was mentioned in the 75th Infantry history: "The intense cold proved as serious an antagonist as the enemy. Non-battle casualties, largely trench foot, frostbite, and cold injury, accounted for 2,623 casualties. The men were not fully prepared for severe winter warfare."[5]

---

[5] U.S. Army. 75th Infantry Division, *The 75th Infantry Division in Combat*, (1945), pp. 3-4.

IN THE SERVICE OF HIS COUNTRY

The Battle of the Bulge – lasting from December 16, 1944 to January 28, 1945 – involved at least a million fighting men, including 600,000 Germans troops, 500,000 Americans, and 55,000 British. By the end of the campaign, the German threat had been eliminated. But the costs had been enormous: 81,000 American casualties with 19,000 killed, 1,400 British casualties with 200 killed, and up to 100,000 Germans killed, wounded or captured.

On January 14, as the 75th Infantry moved across the Salm River near St. Marie, Belgium, to occupy the high wooded ground overlooking the river, the unit was surprised by "a barrage of artillery and mortars" as they approached the crest of the hill. Sergeant MacCarrick wrote that "the suddenness and accuracy of the fire inflicted the greatest number of casualties ever suffered by the [Able] company in a single engagement."[6]

---

[6] Franklin C. MacCarrick, Jr., *op. cit.*, p. 5.

During February 1945, Louie Dominguez and the other men of the 289th Infantry Regiment took part in the American drive through France. In early February, the 75th had reached the Rhine River near the towns of Hetten and Obersaasheim. Having reached the Rhone-Rhine Canal, the 75th felt great pride in the fact that they had chased the German forces clear out of French Alsace. On February 8, its mission along the French side of the Rhine River completed, the Seventy-fifth Infantry Division was relieved of its position and moved north to Panningen, Holland, where they arrived at on February 20. At this time, the 75th was placed under the command of the VIII Corps of the British Second Army. [7]

Reaching the Rhine River

On March 10, 1945, the 75th Division occupied a sector on the west bank of the Rhine, across from Duisberg and Wesel. Their mission was to defend the west bank against any German attacks or patrol activities and "to guard communication lines, utilities,

---

[7] *The 75th Infantry Division in Combat*, (1945), p. 25.

bridges, and culverts; to improve the defensive positions; to dispatch night patrols to the east shore in order to discover the enemy strength, order of battle, and the terrain situation." The 75th was successful in preventing German patrols from crossing the Rhine to engage in reconnaissance activity.[8]

Between March 10 and 24, the Division sent more than thirty patrols organized by three regiments across the Rhine. According to the official 75th Division history, nineteen of these patrols "were able to produce valuable enemy intelligence, including information of enemy strength, dugouts, trenches, pillboxes, wire, observation posts, 88mm guns, antiaircraft, machine gun, mortar and artillery positions. These operations were made hazardous by the river itself, with its cold waters and swift currents; by enemy

---

[8] *Ibid.*, p. 28.

searchlights, and by enemy counter-patrol activities. As a result, several of the patrols suffered casualties."[9]

On March 13th, Sergeant Flores of the 289th Infantry Regiment's A Company led one of these missions across the Rhine. Uncle Louie took part in this reconnaissance patrol. On their way back, however, enemy fire destroyed the kayak in which Privates Sawgle and Peterson were traveling in. Fortunately, Uncle Louie and the other three men in the patrol reached the west bank of the Rhine safely. Finally, on March 29, the 75th Division completed its crossing to the east bank of the Rhine River, officially penetrating German territory.[10]

The Ultimate Sacrifice

On March 31, the 289th stopped short of the small city of Marl, a short distance east of the Rhine River. As they moved forward,

---

[9] *Ibid.*, p. 29.

[10] Franklin C. MacCarrick, Jr. *op. cit.*, p. 17.

they had encountered direct high velocity fire on their flanks.[11]
Then, as they approached a hill on which the Germans were
entrenched, the captain of Louie's unit carefully surveyed the
situation and came to the conclusion that, in order to take this
elevated stronghold, he would have to send an advance unit
forward to locate the enemy's exact position.

When the Captain asked for volunteers, Louie Dominguez quickly
stepped forward. Soon after, Louie and several other soldiers of A
Company advanced up the hill towards the German positions.
Suddenly enemy fire targeted the American soldiers and several of
the soldiers fell to the ground. On this day, five weeks before the
surrender of Nazi Germany, 18-year-old Louie Dominguez died
for his country.

---

[11] *The 75ᵗʰ Infantry Division in Combat*, (1945), p. 31.

A LEGACY OF SERVICE

Honoring the Heroes

In the middle of April, the news about Uncle Louie reached Kansas City. My entire family was devastated, especially because they had no idea whether Uncle Erminio was still alive or not. My parents and my aunts and uncles worried that they may have lost two brothers in this war against tyranny.

On the following page, we have reproduced the Kansas City *Star's* announcement of the death of Louie and the capture of Erminio. Unfortunately, the article contained some inaccuracies, calling Louie a Corporal and stating that his death occurred on March 21st, when in fact, he was killed ten days later. The article also stated that Uncle Erminio was with the 3rd Ranger Division, which was not true. In times of grief and misunderstanding because of language differences, such mistakes were not uncommon.[1]

---

[1] Kansas City *Star*, April 25, 1945.

Army and Navy Official Reports

BROTHERS ARE CASUALTIES.

Louis Dominguez Is Killed—Erminio Dominguez a Prisoner.

Cpl. Louis Dominguez, 18-year-old infantryman, was killed in action in Germany, March 21, it has been learned by his brothers and sisters. His parents are dead.

Corporal Dominguez was graduated from the Turner, Kas., grade school and entered service in August of last year. He went overseas in January.

Louis Dominguez.

A brother, Pfc. Erminio Dominguez, 22, just had been announced a prisoner of the Germans. He went into the army in 1942 and was sent overseas a year ago to the 3d U. S. Rangers.

Corporal Dominguez is survived also by two other brothers, Paul Dominguez, Turner, and Jess Dominguez, 1043 South Twenty-fourth street, Kansas City, Kansas, and two sisters, Mrs. Felica Morales, 1047 South Twenty-sixth street, and Miss Effie Dominguez, Turner.

Erminio Dominguez.

Casualty Announcement, Kansas City Star, April 25, 1945

A LEGACY OF SERVICE

The 75th Infantry Division had spent ninety-four consecutive days in combat and took part in both the Battle of the Bulge (December 23, 1944 to January 28, 1945) and in the Battle of the Colmar Pocket (January 30, 1945 to February 9, 1945). Of equal importance, however, was the Battle for the Ruhr, in which the Allies sought to neutralize "the most highly concentrated industrial area in Europe." The 75th Infantry history states that "with a pre-war population of more than four million," the Ruhr Valley "produced eighty percent of Germany's coal, iron, and steel, and most of its chemicals and synthetic rubber. Its loss would prevent the Reich from long continuing the war."[2]

The Battle for the Ruhr Valley of Germany began on March 31, 1945 – the day that my Uncle Louie was killed in action – and lasted until April 15, 1945. The official history of the 75th Infantry states that "the operation was carried out against formidable obstacles" and that the 75th Division's "mission called for the

---

[2] *The 75th Infantry Division in Combat*, (1945), p. 26.

highest exertion of all arms." By the time that the Ruhr was neutralized, the 75th had taken 3,654 German prisoners and liberated 2,132 Allied prisoners of war. From April16 to May 21, as their role became occupational, the 75th took 14,173 prisoners of war.[3]

During its ninety-four days in combat, the 75th Infantry had the following losses: 817 soldiers killed in action (KIA), 3,314 wounded in action, and 111 who died of wounds, representing almost 60% of the total unit strength.[4] The 75th captured 20,630 German soldiers. For its combat participation in World War II, the soldiers of the 75th Division received numerous awards, including four Distinguished Service Crosses, 193 Silver Stars, 7 Legion of Merits, 30 Soldier's Medals, and 1321 Bronze Star Medals. For his own military service, Uncle Louie posthumously

[3] *Ibid.*, pp. 26-27.

[4] Horst Hassel, "75th Infantry Division (WWII): History from 1943 to 1995" Online: <http://www.plbg.de/75th/history.htm>. [Last updated August 5, 2001.]

received six medals, including the bronze star, the Purple Heart and the combat infantry badge.

The Liberation of Moosburg

At the time of Uncle Louie's death on March 31, 1945, Uncle Erminio Dominguez was still interned at the Moosburg POW Camp (Stalag VIIA) in the Bavarian state of Germany. Many POWs from other parts of Germany had been transferred to Stalag VIIA at this late stage of the war.

Being held as a POW for any period of time is a traumatic experience and even when a man is released from captivity, he carries around the memories of his imprisonment like a "black cloud." The nightmares keep coming back, even many years after freedom has been restored. As a means of forgetting this terrible chapter in their lives, many POWs refuse to talk about their experiences. This was the case for Uncle Erminio.

Shortly after returning home, Erminio had told his brother Jesse that some of the German guards had treated the American prisoners like animals, sometimes throwing their food to them like they would throw meat to a dog. After this short revelation, Erminio never talked about his war experiences ever again, not to his wife, his children, or to other family members.

However, Mr. Bill Ethridge was an American POW who was transferred to Moosburg on April 21, 1945 in the last days of the war. It is through Mr. Ethridge's memoirs that we have been given some idea of the last days of Erminio Dominguez' captivity in Moosburg. Mr. Ethridge's first impressions of the camp, detailed in his memoirs, *Time Out: A Remembrance of World War II*, were not good: [5]

> The camp was a mess. As far as we could see throughout the camp there was nothing but mud and

---

[5] Bill Ethridge, "Time Out. A Remembrance of World War II." (1998), pp. 137-143; Moosburg WebTeam, "Stalag VII A: Oral History: Part II: Stalag VII-A Moosburg" Online: <http://www.moosburg.org/info/stalag/eth2eng.html>. [Last updated May 12, 2000].

hundreds and hundreds of prisoners. The first order of business was to register. Record-keeping was a fetish with our hosts. All of our names and prior camps had to be listed and verified.

When Mr. Ethridge and the other soldiers learned that they were being transferred to a POW camp that was only twenty-five or so kilometers from Munich, they were very happy. Some of the prisoners had learned from clandestine radios that the Third Army of General George S. Patton's army was racing through Bavaria en route to Munich. It was highly likely that they would see the American forces within days.[6]

For the period April 22 to April 27, Mr. Ethridge observed that "This camp is much worse than we had expected. Everything is pretty disorganized and the Germans are arrogant and edgy... There is no wood available for use by the prisoners in their small

---

[6] Bill Ethridge, *op. cit.*, pp. 125-136; Moosburg WebTeam, "Stalag VII A: Oral History: Part I: The Road to Bavaria." Online: <http://www.moosburg.org/info/stalag/eth1eng.html>. [Last updated May 12, 2000].

make-shift stoves. To make matters worse, the grounds are ankle-deep in mud despite the fact that it rained only one day this week! We were informed that this had been a swamp at one time and that it was always wet." [7]

Then, on April 28th, Mr. Ethridge writes "We could hear artillery fire in the distance coming from the west and southwest. This is the direction that General Patton is supposedly coming from. I hope!... Everybody is on edge, expecting that Patton will take the camp any time. The Germans are also sure of that... There was very little sleeping tonight. We were mentally helping Patton come through. We could hear the artillery getting closer by the minute and the resulting sounds and the vibrations reminded me of a Midwest thunder storm."[8]

---

[7] Bill Ethridge, *op. cit.*; Moosburg WebTeam, "Stalag VII A: Oral History: Part II: Stalag VII-A Moosburg" Online: <http://www.moosburg.org/info/stalag/eth2eng.html>. [Last updated May 12, 2000].

[8] *Ibid.*

Then, on April 29, 1945 Combat Team A of the 14th Armored Division appeared near the camp entrance. The German guards did not offer resistance. The American flag went up at Moosburg at 12:15 PM. Finally, at 1:45 P.M., several jeeps and tanks rolled into the camp and received a deafening ovation.[9] Bill Ethridge, recounting the day of liberation, wrote:[10]

> Daybreak brought the sound of shouting and gunfire at the front gate. From our barracks we could see German troops near that gate, and they were firing in! We were ordered to stay inside as the Germans began fighting each other. We found out later when bodies were being loaded onto a truck that the Gestapo had attempted to take the camp from the Wehrmacht [German Army]. Little did we know at that time, but Hitler had issued an order to kill all of the prisoners in the camp. The Gestapo and the SS troops attempted to carry out that Order, and the German army had saved our lives. Almost on cue after the fighting stopped, American troops backed by one tank and one Jeep arrived at the front gate. The

---

[9] Hell's Angels, 303rd Bomb Group (H) Association, "German POW Camps with 303rd BG(H) Prisoners (1998-2003). Online: <http://www.303rdbga.com/pow-camps.html#stalag7a>. [Last updated July 3, 2003.]

[10] Bill Ethridge, *op. cit.*; Moosburg WebTeam, "Stalag VII A: Oral History: Part II: Stalag VII-A Moosburg" Online: <http://www.moosburg.org/info/stalag/eth2eng.html>. [Last updated May 12, 2000].

German army personnel surrendered immediately. The American flag was raised over Moosburg at 1240 hours, and it was a sight that brought tears to many eyes. At 1315, General Patton came through the gate, standing erect in his Jeep behind his driver. Another Jeep followed with four heavily armed soldiers. There, finally, was Old Blood and Guts in person with those famous pistols on his hips. Tears were rolling down hundreds of faces including mine. The memories and the visions of this day will live with me forever.

General Patton gave a speech to the liberated prisoners and then added: "We will whip the bastards all the way to Berlin." Moosburg was the last of the POW camps to be liberated and, with their newfound freedom, some 90,000 American ex-POWs, prepared to return to their homes in the United States. Nine days later, on May 8, 1945, Germany unconditionally surrendered to the Allied forces.

With these events, my Uncle Erminio became a free man. The brave veteran of the French and Italian campaigns received a warm welcome from the Dominguez family in Kansas City.

A LEGACY OF SERVICE

However, when Erminio found out that his younger brother Louie had died in combat just a few weeks earlier, his sense of loss was overwhelming.

Although Erminio received four bronze stars, the Purple Heart, the service ribbon and a good conduct medal for his extraordinary service to his country, he never spoke of his experiences in World War II to anyone ever again. However, proud to have served his country, Erminio eventually became a member of the Kansas City VFW. Two years after being released from German captivity, Erminio Dominguez was married to Carmen Garcia, the half-sister of my father, Daniel Morales. For the rest of his life, Erminio worked as a forklift operator for the Santa Fe Railroad. On June 8, 1996, Erminio Dominguez died at the age of 74.

The Double Standard

Esperanza Rangel, in her anguish, struggled to understand the loss of her childhood friend, Louie Dominguez, and pondered over the meaning of his death in battlefield action. Many years later, reflecting on Uncle Louie's service to his country, she wrote:[11]

> Statistics say that Mexican Americans died completely disproportionate to our numbers. Yet, depressingly enough, social policies for minorities in war and in peace were a double standard. Overseas, military death had no restrictions; all were entitled. The battlefields took their claim uncaring about the heritage of man, its crimson saturations untelling if shed by black, white, brown, red or yellow man. Back home, life itself was not so charitable.

World War II represented a bittersweet experience for Mexican-American men in Kansas and the nation as a whole. Although they had helped win the war through their important contributions, Mexican-American soldiers returning from overseas were discriminated against in education, employment, and public accommodations. When she witnessed these injustices to her brothers and other Hispanics in Kansas City, Esperanza felt outrage and disgust.

---

[11] Esperanza Amayo, "All Equal in Death," Kansas City *Star*, June 3, 1984.

For some time, she even questioned the validity of the sacrifices of Mexican Americans in war, feeling that these contributions were not appreciated by some Americans. When she heard that Louie had been killed in action, Esperanza was told by her neighbors and friends that "Louie died in the name of peace and liberty." And yet, in an interview with the authors, she observed, "Mexican-American servicemen returning to Kansas from World War II did not earn an ounce of respect for their war duties and sacrifices. Instead of a confetti and ticker-tape welcome, these conquering heroes were blatantly denied the liberties and ordinary human rights guaranteed to Anglos."

Discrimination against my people continued well into the 1950s. Esperanza told the authors that Mexican-American veterans were refused membership to the local American Legion Post 111 for many years. But, she pointed out, "our veterans refused to be deterred by this blatant and insulting rejection. Instead, they formed their own American Legion Post 213."

A LEGACY OF SERVICE

The determination of these "retired" warriors would gradually bring about changes. So it can be said that World War II and its aftermath marked an important political and social turning point for Mexican Americans in Kansas and around the whole country. A whole generation of Mexican-American men took advantage of the G.I. bill to get an education. And with an education, these men would learn how to make the system work in their favor. These men questioned the old system that tolerated discrimination and segregation. And, over time, things did change.

Proudly, Esperanza told the authors that "Mexican-American veterans fought for the privileges of good citizenship that Anglos took for granted. They worked hard to better their own lives and to challenge the negative stereotypes that many Americans had of Mexican Americans. Today, these men and their children can stand tall and proud of their contributions in both war and peace."

A LEGACY OF SERVICE

Over the years, Esperanza saw a change in attitudes and a new appreciation of the contributions of Mexican Americans. Half a century after the end of World War II, Esperanza wrote in the Kansas City *Star* that "we in this country were free to struggle and rise above our adversities. And now in this era of racial justice, I finally know that indeed my friend did die for me. His memory will live with me always."[12]

The Value of Citizenship

I was born after World War II but today, having studied the struggles and triumphs of my family in Kansas City, I have an appreciation for what they did for me. Citizenship is bestowed upon any person born on American soil. All but two of the children of Geronimo Dominguez and Luisa Lujan were born in the United States and were, therefore, citizens of the U.S.

---

[12] Esperanza Amayo, "All Equal in Death," Kansas City *Star*, June 3, 1984.

A LEGACY OF SERVICE

But when my family came to Kansas City toward the end of World War I, they learned that being accepted as Americans was not so easy. As the testimony of Esperanza and others has indicated, Mexican Americans were – for the most part – treated like second-class citizens.

To my people – working the railroads and laboring in the sugar beet fields of Nebraska – there was never any doubt about our place in America. The Dominguez family sent their children to school, paid their taxes, worked in the defense industry and for the railroads, and became involved in church activities. We carried on and made the best of things.

When my uncles went to war, they went with the dedication of knowing that – in some great way – they were defending their native land and safeguarding the freedom and future of their family and of all Americans. World War II became a testing ground for our loyalty, and we passed the text with flying colors.

A LEGACY OF SERVICE

My uncles, with great pride and determination, served their country in a time of need. They are merely two among many who served proudly. It is believed that some 500,000 Mexican Americans served in the armed forces during World War II. And this legacy of service would continue.

Erminio and Louie Dominguez served as role models for my family. Five years after the end of World War II, my cousin Eleno Salazar, Jr., served in the Korean War. In the years to follow, many family members, including my daughter Gina, have enlisted in the armed forces and served their country. Today, I realize that when my Uncle Louie died on that hill in Germany, he paid for my freedom and he paid for the freedom of all Americans. I will remain forever grateful for his service.

The Dominguez family has been in the United States for ninety-four years and in that period of time, we have earned an important place in American society. In seeking to convey to you my feelings about my family, I will once again borrow the words of family friend, Esperanza Amayo. Discussing the Mexican-American community of Kansas City with the authors, Esperanza explained that "there is a grace to our achievements because, in spite of educational barriers and the subjugation of job restraints, Mexican-Americans in this area prevailed. We contributed in war and in peace to the productivity and stability of the Kansas City community and we now enjoy a self-fulfilling and respectable place in its society."

BIBLIOGRAPHY

102nd Cavalry. *Reconnaissance Squadron, 102nd Cavalry Reconnaissance Squadron, World War II.*. Short   Hills, New Jersey, 1983.

117th Cavalry. *The Operational History of the 117th Cavalry Reconnaissance Squadron (Mechanized), World War II.* Westfield, New Jersey: 117th Cavalry Assn, 1982.

1920 Kansas City Directory and Business Catalog. Kansas City: Gale City Directory Company, 1920.

Acosta-Belen, Edna and Barbara R. Sjostrom, eds. *The Hispanic Experience in the United States: Contemporary Issues and Perspectives*. New York: Praeger Publishers, 1988.

Agueyo, José. "Los Betabeleros (The Beetworkers)." In *La Gente: Hispano History and Life in Colorado*. Edited by Vincent C. DeBaca, pp. 105-119. Denver: Colorado Historical Society, 1998.

Alford, Harold. *The Proud Peoples: The Heritage and Culture of Spanish-Speaking Peoples in the United States*. New York: David McKay, 1972.

BIBLIOGRAPHY

Altman, Ida and Lockhart, James. *Provinces of Early Mexico: Variants of Spanish American Regional Evolution.* Los Angeles: UCLA Latin American Center Publications, University of California, Los Angeles, 1976.

Amayo, Esperanza. "Despite Sting of Past Abuses, Mexican-Americans Endure," Kansas City *Star*, Nov. 19, 1980.

Amayo, Esperanza. "All Equal in Death," Kansas City *Star*, June 3, 1984.

Amayo, Esperanza. "Be Proud of Immigrants," Kansas City *Kansan*, Feb. 1, 1995.

Amayo, Esperanza. "Mexican-American Vets Deserve to be Honored," Kansas City *Star*, May 5, 1995, p. C7.

Amayo, Esperanza. "Mexican-Americans' Roots Have Grown Deep in County," Kansas City *Star*, June 12, 1997, p.2

Anna, Timothy E. *Forging Mexico, 1821-1835.* Lincoln, Nebraska: University of Nebraska Press, 1998.

BIBLIOGRAPHY

Anderson, Esther S. *The Sugar Beet Industry of Nebraska* –Bulletin 9, Conservation Department of the Conservation and Survey Division. Lincoln, Nebraska: University of Nebraska (April, 1935), pp. 25-27.

Avila, Henry J. "Immigration and Integration: The Mexican American Community in Garden City, Kansas, 1900-1950." *Kansas History* 20 (Spring 1997): pp. 22-37.

Bakewell, P. J. *Silver Mining and Society in Colonial Mexico: Zacatecas, 1546-1700.* Cambridge: Cambridge University Press, 1971.

Balderrama, Francisco E., and Raymond Rodríguez. *Decade of Betrayal: Mexican Repatriation in the 1930s.* Albuquerque: University of New Mexico Press, 1995.

Barnett, Lana Payne and Elizabeth Brooks Buhrkuhl, eds. *Presenting the Texas Panhandle.* Canyon, Texas: Lan-Bea, 1979.

Bean, Frank D., and Marta Tienda. *The Hispanic Population of the United States.* New York: Russell Sage Foundation, 1987.

BIBLIOGRAPHY

Bernal, Martha E. and Phylis C. Martinelli, eds. *Mexican American Identity*. Encino, Ca.: Floricanto, 1993.

Bogardus, Emory S. *The Mexican in the United States*. Los Angeles: University of Southern California, 1934.

Borjas, George J. and Marta Tienda, eds. *Hispanics in the U.S. Economy*. Orlando: Academic Press, 1985.

Browning, Harley L. and Rodolfo O. de la Garza, eds. *Mexican Immigrants and Mexican Americans: An Evolving Relation*. Austin: University of Texas, Austin, Center for Mexican American Studies, 1986.

Cadenhead, Ivie E. *Jesús González Ortega and Mexican National Politics* – Texas Christian University Monographs in History and Culture, No. 9. Fort Worth: the Texas Christian University Press, 1972.

Cárdenas, Gilbert. "Los Desarraigados: Chicanos in the Midwestern Region of the United States." *Aztlán* 7:2 (1976): pp. 153-186.

BIBLIOGRAPHY

Cardoso, Lawrence A. *Mexican Emigration to the United States, 1897-1931*. Tucson: University of Arizona Press, 1980.

Carman, J. Neale. *Foreign-Language Units of Kansas: I. Historical Atlas and Statistics*. Lawrence, Kansas: University of Kansas Press, 1962.

Carranza, Miguel A. "The Hispanic Presence on the Great Plains: An Introduction." *Great Plains Quarterly* 10 (Spring 1990): pp. 67-70.

Carter, Thomas P. *Mexican Americans in School: A History of Educational Neglect*. New York: College Entrance Examination Board, 1970.

Cockcroft, James D. *Mexico: Class Formation, Capital Accumulation, and the State*. New York: Monthly Review Press, 1983.

Cole, Hugh M. *The Ardennes: Battle of the Bulge*. Washington: Government Printing Office, 1965

BIBLIOGRAPHY

Corwin, Arthur F., ed. *Immigrants—And Immigrants: Perspectives on Mexican Labor Migration to the United States.* Westport: Greenwood Press, 1978.

Corwin, Arthur F. "Mexican Emigration History, 1900-1970: Literature and Research," *Latin American Research Review,* VIII (Summer 1973), pp. 3-24.

Corwin, Arthur F. "Early Mexican Labor Migration: A Frontier Sketch, 1848-1900," in *Immigrants – and Immigrants: Perspectives on Mexican Labor Migration to the United States,* Arthur F. Corwin, ed. Westport, Conn.: Greenwood, 1979.

Crocchiola, Stanley F. *Rodeo Town (Canadian, Texas).* Denver: World, 1953.

Dorsett, Lyle. *The Pendergast Machine.* Lincoln: University of Nebraska Press, 1968.

Dunne, Peter Masten. *Pioneer Jesuits in Northern Mexico.* Berkeley: University of California Press, 1944.

Duran, Livie I., and H. Russell Bernard (eds). *Introduction to Chicano Studies.* New York: Macmillan, 1982.

Esposito, Vincent J. (ed.). *West Point Atlas of American Wars*. New York: Frderick A. Praeger, Publishers, 1959.

Estrada, Leobardo F. "A Demographic Comparison of the Mexican Origin Population in the Midwest and Southwest." *Aztlán* 7:2 (1976): pp. 203-234.

Ethridge, Bill. "Stalag VII A: Oral History: Part I: The Road to Bavaria." Online: [Last updated May 12, 2000]: <http://www.moosburg.org/info/stalag/eth1eng.html>.

Ethridge, Bill. "Time Out. A Remembrance of World War II." "Stalag VII A: Oral History: Part II: Stalag VII-A Moosburg." Online: [Last updated May 12, 2000]. <http://www.moosburg.org/info/stalag/eth2eng.html>.

Funk & Wagnalls Corporation. *The World Almanac and Book of Facts, 1995*. Mahwah, New Jersey: Funk & Wagnalls Corporation, 1994.

Gamio, Manuel. *Mexican Immigration to the United States*. Chicago: The University of Chicago Press, 1930.

BIBLIOGRAPHY

García, Juan R, (ed.). *Community, Identity, and Education*. Tucson: Mexican American Studies and Research Center, *Perspectives in Mexican American Studies* No. 3, 1992.

García, Juan R. *Mexicans in the Midwest, 1900-1932*. Tucson: University of Arizona Press, 1996.

García, Juan R. *Mexicans in the Midwest*. Tucson: Mexican American Studies and Research Center, *Perspectives in Mexican American Studies* No. 2, 1989.

Gerhard, Peter. *The Northern Frontier of New Spain*. Princeton, New Jersey: Princeton University Press, 1982.

Gonzales, Louis. *The Dominguez – Chavez Family History*. Kansas City, 2000.

Gonzales, Louis. *Dominguez: Footsteps in Time*. Kansas City, 2003.

Gonzáles, Manuel G. *Mexicanos: A History of Mexicans in the United States*. Bloomington: Indiana University Press, 1999.

BIBLIOGRAPHY

Gradie, Charlotte M. *The Tepehuan Revolt of 1616: Militarism, Evangelism, and Colonialism in Seventeenth-Century Nueva Vizcaya*. Salt Lake City: The University of Utah Press, 2000.

Grajedia, Ralph F. "Mexicans in Nebraska," (Lincoln, Nebraska: Nebraska State Historical Society, 1998) [Updated Oct 5, 1998.]. Accessed online at: <http://www.nebraskahistory.org/lib-arch/whadoin/mexampub/mexicans.htm>.

Green, Stanley C. *The Mexican Republic: The First Decade, 1823-1832*. Pittsburgh: The University of Pittsburgh Press, 1987.

Hassel, Horst. *75th Infantry Division (WWII): History from 1943 to 1995*. Online: <http://www.plbg.de/75th/history.htm>. [Last updated August 5, 2001.]

Hoffman, Abraham. *Unwanted Mexican Americans in the Great Depression: Repatriation Pressure, 1929-1939*. Tucson: University of Arizona Press, 1974.

BIBLIOGRAPHY

Hoffman, Dorothy Elizabeth. *Service Rendered to Mexican Groups in Kansas City, Missouri Through the Guadalupe Center.* Master's Thesis: University of Missouri, 1938.

Instituto Nacional de Estadística Geografía e Informática (INEGI). *Estados Unidos Mexicanos. Conteo de Población y Vivienda, 1995*

INEGI. *Tabulados Básicos. Estados Unidos Mexicanos. XII Censo General de Población y Vivienda, 2000.* México, 2001.

INEGI, *Superficies Nacionales y Estatales.* 1999. Inédito.

Jiménez, Carlos M. *The Mexican American Heritage.* Berkeley, California: TQS Publications, 1994 (2nd edition).

Kansas Ethnic Council. *The Ethnic History of Wyandotte County.* Kansas City: Kansas Ethnic Council, 1992.

Kerr, John Leeds and Frank Donovan. *Destination Topolobampo: The Kansas City, Mexico & Orient Railway.* San Marino, California: Golden West Books, 1968.

BIBLIOGRAPHY

Key, Della Tyler. *In the Cattle Country: History of Potter County, 1887-1966.* Wichita Falls: Nortex, 1972.

Kirchhoff, Paul. "The Hunting-Gathering People of North Mexico," in Basil C. Hedrick et al. (ed.), *The North Mexican Frontier: Readings in Archaeology, Ethnohistory, and Ethnography* (Carbondale, Illinois: Southern Illinois University Press, 1971).

Laird, Judith Fincher. *Argentine, Kansas: The Evolution of a Mexican-American Community, 1905-1940* Dissertation: University of Kansas, 1975. Ann Arbor, Michigan: University Microfilms International, 1979.

Leonard, Edward A. *Rails at the Pass of the North* – Southwestern Studies Monograph No. 63. El Paso: Texas Western Press, 1981.

MacDonald, Charles B. *The Last Offensive.* United States in World War II. Washington: Government Printing Office, 1973

Massey, Douglas Steven. *Residential Segregation of Spanish Americans in the United States.* Dissertation: Princeton University, 1978.

BIBLIOGRAPHY

McDaniel, Ted (ed.). *Our Land: A History of Lyon County Kansas*. Emporia: Emporia State Press, 1976.

McNeely, John H. *The Railways of Mexico: A Study in Nationalization* – Southwestern Studies No. 5. El Paso: Texas Western Press, 1964.

McWilliams, Carey. *North from Mexico: The Spanish-Speaking People of the United States*. New York: Greenwood Press, 1968.

Mecham, J. Lloyd. *Francisco de Ibarra and Neuva Vizcaya*. Durham, North Carolina, Duke University Press, 1927.

Meier, Matt S., and Feliciano Rivera. *Mexican Americans/American Mexicans: From Conquistadores to Chicanos*. New York: Hill and Wang, 1993.

Mendoza, Valerie M. "They Came to Kansas: Searching for a Better Life." *Kansas Quarterly* 25 (No. 2, 1994): pp. 97-106.

Mendoza, Valerie M. *The Creation of a Mexican Immigrant Community in Kansas City, 1890-1930*. Dissertation: University of California, Berkeley, 1997.

BIBLIOGRAPHY

Mexican Central Railway Company Limited. *Facts and Figures About Mexico and Her Great Railroad, The Mexican Central.* Mexico City: Mexican Central Railway Company Limited, 1900 – Third edition.

"MEXLIST: The Mexican List for Railroad Information: USA - Mexico railroad gateways and related trackage," http://mexican.railspot.com/minsk2.htm. Updated January 12, 2003. Accessed June 8, 2003.

Mines, Cynthia. *Riding the Rails to Kansas: The Mexican Immigrants.* McPherson, Kansas: 1980.

Monroy, Douglas. *Rebirth: Mexican Los Angeles from the Great Migration to the Great Depression.* Berkeley: University of California Press, 1999.

Oppenheimer, Robert. "Acculturation or Assimilation: Mexican Immigrants in Kansas, 1900 to World War II." *Western Historical Quarterly* 16:4 (1985): pp. 429-448.

BIBLIOGRAPHY

Parlee, Lorena M. *Porfirio Diaz, Railroads, and Development in Northern Mexico: A Study of Government Policy Toward the Central and Nacional Railroads, 1876-1910.* Ann Arbor, Michigan: University Microfilms International, 1981.

Powell, Philip Wayne,. *Soldiers, Indians and Silver: North America's First Frontier War.* Tempe, Arizona: Center for Latin American Studies, Arizona State University, 1973.

Priestley, Herbert Ingram. *The Mexican Nation, A History.* New York: The Macmillan Company, 1926.

Reddy, Marlita A., ed. *Statistical Record of Hispanic Americans.* Detroit: Gale Research, Inc., 1993.

Reisler, Mark. *By the Sweat of Their Brow: Mexican Immigrant Labor in the United States, 1900-1940.* Westport: Greenwood Press, 1976.

Rosales, Francisco Arturo. *Mexican Immigration to the Urban Midwest During the 1920s.* Dissertation: Indiana University, 1978.

BIBLIOGRAPHY

Rutter, Larry G. "Mexican Americans in Kansas: a Survey and Social Mobility Study, 1900-1970." Master's Thesis, Kansas State University, 1972.

Samsel, Harold J. *The Battle of Montrevel, France, September 3, 1944: 117th Cavalry Reconnaissance Squadron (Mechanized)*. 2nd Ed. Princeton, NJ: Triangle Repro, 1986.

Samsel, Harold J. *Operational History of the 102nd Cavalry Regiment (Group) "Essex Troop", 38th Cavalry*. Westfield, New Jersey: 117th Cavalry Association, 1982.

Sánchez, George I. *Forgotten People: A Study of New Mexicans*. Albuquerque: University of New Mexico Press, 1940.

Sánchez, George. *Becoming Mexican American: Ethnicity, Culture, and Identity in Chicano Los Angeles, 1900 – 1945*. New York: Oxford University Press, 1993.

Schirmer, Sherry Lamb. *Historical Overview of the Ethnic Communities in Kansas City*. Kansas City, Missouri: Pan-Educational Institute, 1976.

BIBLIOGRAPHY

Schmal, John P. *The Morales-Dominguez Family History.* Los Angeles, California, 2000.

Schmal, John P. "The History of Hispanics in America's Defense," www.*somosPrimos.com* (July 2000, Issue 7).

Schmal, John P. and Donna S. Morales, *My Family Through Time.* Los Angeles, California, 2000.

Schmal, John P. and Donna S. Morales, *Mexican-American Genealogical Research: Following the Paper Trail to Mexico."* Bowie, Maryland: Heritage Books, Inc., 2002.

Smith, Michael M. "Beyond the Borderlands: Mexican Labor in the Central Plains, 1900-1930." *Great Plains Quarterly* 1:4 (1981): pp. 239-251.

Smith, Michael M. "Mexicans in Kansas City: The First Generation, 1900-1920." In *Mexicans in the Midwest*, ed. Juan R. García, 29-57. *Perspectives in Mexican American Studies*, No. 2. Tucson: Mexican American Studies and Research Center, 1989.

BIBLIOGRAPHY

Smith, Michael M. "The Mexican Immigrant Press Beyond the Borderlands: The Case of El Cosmopolita, 1914-19." *Great Plains Quarterly* 10 (Spring 1990): pp. 71-85.

Sotomayor, Elsie. *Historical Aspects Related to the Assimilation and Acculturation of the Mexican-American People, 1848-1920.* Master's Thesis: California State University, Fullerton, 1976.

Stover, John F. *The Routledge Historical Atlas of the American Railroads: Routledge Atlases of American History.* New York: Routledge, 1999.

Taylor, Paul S. "Some Aspects of Mexican Immigration," *Journal of Political Economy* 38 (October 1930).

Taylor, Paul S. *Mexican Labor in the United States.* New York: Arno Press and *New York Times*, 1970.

U.S. Bureau of Census. *The Statistical History of the United States from Colonial Times to the Present.* Stamford, Conn.: Fairfield Publishers, Inc., 1947.